The Big Picture

Other Books by John Hilton III and Anthony Sweat

Why? Powerful Answers and Practical Reasons
for Living LDS Standards

How? Essential Skills for Living the Gospel

The Big Picture

*20 Family-Friendly Lessons
on God's Plan for You*

John Hilton III and Anthony Sweat

DESERET
BOOK

Salt Lake City, Utah

Library of Congress Cataloging-in-Publication Data

Hilton, John, III, author.
  The big picture : 20 family-friendly lessons on God's plan for you / John Hilton III and Anthony Sweat.
      pages   cm
  Includes bibliographical references.
  ISBN 978-1-60907-176-9 (paperbound)
1. Plan of salvation (Mormon theology)   2. Mormon cosmology.   3. Christian life—Mormon authors.   4. The Church of Jesus Christ of Latter-day Saints—Doctrines.
5. Mormon Church—Doctrines.   I. Sweat, Anthony, author.   II. Title.
  BX8643.S25H55 2012
  230'.9332—dc23   2012029530

Printed in the United States of America
Malloy Lithographing Incorporated, Ann Arbor, MI

10   9   8   7   6   5   4   3   2   1

We dedicate this book
to the Hilton and Sweat children.
We try to teach you all about life, and
you teach us what life is all about.

A testimony of the plan of salvation
can give you hope and purpose as you wrestle
with the challenges of life.

—*True to the Faith*

Contents

Act III: Life after Death

Acknowledgments

Our gratitude goes to the team at Deseret Book: Heidi Taylor, for overseeing this project from start to finish and making it happen. The book wouldn't exist without you. Chris Schoebinger, for supporting us from the very beginning. This book is an extension of your genius behind *Why?* and *How?* Lisa Mangum, for your editorial acumen that smoothed out our rough spots, and for your timeline talents that kept the project on track. Shauna Gibby, for your tireless design and layout work, including the cover. Tonya Facemyer and Rachael Ward, for typesetting a book that isn't so easy to typeset. To each of you we give our sincerest thanks for contributions in bringing this work to fruition.

Preface

This book can be used in two ways.

First, this is a book written for teenagers to sit down and read. If you're a teenager reading this book, great! You are who we are writing to! We hope this book provides you with additional knowledge and insights about God's plan so that you can go forward and use those truths to guide your everyday life. We promise you that you will be blessed as you follow "the great plan of happiness" (Alma 42:8).

Second, this is also a book that parents and teachers can use as a resource when teaching the gospel. Because this book is written to teenagers, perhaps the best thing you can do is to hand it to your child and ask him or her to plan the lesson! As you go through each chapter, you'll periodically find three different kinds of icons.

The Teach the Plan icon that includes a number on it. We refer back to these icons at the end of each chapter where we have provided a lesson outline to help you teach the material in family settings, church, or mutual.

In every chapter, you'll also see the Experiment upon the Word icon. It identifies a hands-on activity that you can do to help you "experiment upon [the word]" (Alma 32:27) and learn more about God's plan for you.

Each chapter also includes a Live the Plan icon that invites you to act on the truths of the plan you are learning.

We know that true doctrine, understood, has the power to change attitudes and behavior. Our sincere desire is that this book can assist you in teaching youth to understand the vital doctrines that are a part of the plan of salvation.

Introduction

The "Big Picture" of the Plan of Salvation

 If you were lost in a dense forest or jungle and could go a thousand feet in any direction, which direction would you go to help you find your way? North, south, east, or west?

Actually, the best direction to go would be a thousand feet straight up. Such a move would help you gain a big-picture perspective of the terrain around you and you could know which way you should go.

Similarly, some people are metaphorically lost in the jungle of life—not knowing which way to turn to find lasting peace and happiness, not understanding the purpose of life, and sometimes not even knowing what is right or wrong. With a limited view, some things in this life can seem confusing, unfair, and uncertain. But when we look heavenward, we are able to gain better perspective and find answers. As we pull back and see the big picture, as we more fully understand God's plan of salvation for us, we can more easily understand why things happen, how we should act, and what we should do to find our way in life.

A Three-Act Play

 Have you ever sat down in the middle of a movie and been totally confused by what is going on? President Boyd K. Packer likened this feeling to our mortal life. He said:

> The plan of redemption, with its three divisions, might be likened to a grand three-act play. Act I is entitled "Premortal Life."
> ... Act II, from birth to the time of resurrection, the "Second

Estate." And Act III, "Life after Death or Immortality Eternal Life."

In mortality, we are like one who enters a theater just as the curtain goes up on the second act. We have missed Act I. The production has many plots and sub-plots that interweave, making it difficult to figure out who relates to whom and what relates to what, who are the heroes and who are the villains. It is further complicated because you are not just a spectator; you are a member of the cast, on stage, in the middle of it all![1]

 Scan this QR code or go to http:// delivr.com/1k77m to see an example of what it might feel like to jump into the middle of a play and how it relates to the plan of salvation.

The Big Picture

The plan of salvation is God's plan "to enable each of us to enjoy all His blessings."[2] If somebody asked you to draw a big-picture overview of God's plan of salvation, what would you draw? What about something like this?[3]

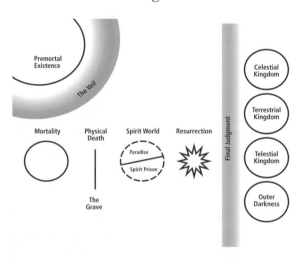

While this picture does not fully capture everything about the plan of salvation, there are some good things about it. It paints in broad strokes the history and destiny of mankind: We lived with God in a premortal existence. After having passed through the veil of forgetfulness, we are now on earth, experiencing mortality without being able to remember our life in the premortal existence. At the end of our mortal life, we will die, and, depending on what we've done and become in our lifetime, we will go to either spirit paradise or spirit prison. Eventually, we will all be resurrected (become immortal with a body of flesh and bone), be judged, and be assigned to a kingdom where we will live forever after.

But there are other ways we can draw the big picture of the plan of salvation. What about this one?

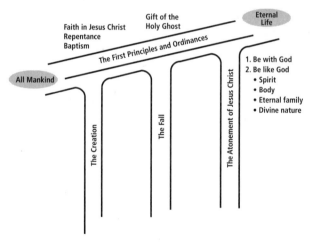

This drawing emphasizes different aspects of the plan of salvation. It shows what have been called "the three pillars of eternity"[4]— the creation of the world, the fall of Adam and Eve, and the atonement of Jesus Christ. These were crucial events in the history of the world, and very important to our personal, eternal progression. Because of these pillars, we can continue on the straight and narrow path through the principles and ordinances of the gospel, and return to live with God. The far right-hand side of this diagram shows the ultimate purposes of God's plan for us: "Eternal Life," or to be with God and become like Him.

Here's yet another "big picture" view of the plan:

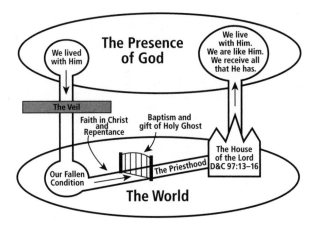

This picture helps us see that we are trying to get from where we are now (our fallen condition) back to the presence of God (where we once were) to receive all His blessings, live with Him, and be like Him. It shows we can do that through Christ and the ordinances of the priesthood.

While each of these diagrams are helpful in their own way, they can sometimes be confusing. There are a lot of circles, lines, arrows, and images. There are many topics and doctrines that often aren't fully explained in the visual presentations: our premortal existence, the Creation, the Fall, Jesus' Atonement, faith, baptism, temple covenants, the spirit world, resurrection, celestial kingdom. And sometimes in the middle of all the circles and lines and topics and doctrines, we can also overlook the whole purpose of life—we can miss out on the very point of the plan of salvation. Like the proverbial saying goes, we can't see the forest because of all the trees.

What Is the Overall Purpose of the Plan of Salvation?

 In five words and with only one arrow, here is a simple summary of the plan of salvation that we feel gets to the heart of the plan:

Premortal Spirit ━━━━━━▶ Become like God
(start)   (end)

God has said that His work and glory is "to bring to pass the immortality and eternal life of man" (Moses 1:39). Eternal life means God's life, or becoming like our Heavenly Father and living a life full of joy. President Joseph F. Smith taught, "We must become like [God]. . . . This is the object of our existence in the world."[5] And President Lorenzo Snow summarized the plan of salvation so beautifully when he declared: "As God is now, man may be."[6] Understanding that the overall purpose of life is to become like our Heavenly Father helps us better understand the "why" of life and know the "how" about things we must do. We start to understand that this life is a test—a test to determine if we will live a life like God's and therefore enjoy all His blessings.

Once we have this main idea fixed in our mind—that God is trying to help us become more like Him—all other aspects of the plan of salvation begin to make more sense and fall into place. The purpose of this book is to get beyond all the circles, lines, and images and help explain the different aspects of God's plan—most important, how the truths of the plan of salvation can give us power and purpose and perspective in our everyday living. In the midst of the jungle of mortality, this book attempts to help us rise a thousand feet heavenward and get an eternal view of God's divine plan of salvation for our life.

We Should Study and Live the Plan of Salvation

The Prophet Joseph Smith taught that the plan of salvation "is a subject we ought to study more than any other. We ought to study it day and night."[7]

And Elder Bruce R. McConkie said, "As rapidly as we learn the plan of salvation and get ourselves in tune with the Holy Spirit . . . our whole souls will be filled with light and understanding."[8]

 Scan this QR code or visit http://www .youtube.com/watch?v=epNjOrfmdlA to watch "We Can Find Happiness"—a video of people who have found happiness from studying and living God's plan of salvation.

It isn't enough to just study about the plan of salvation. We have to *live* it too. Did you know that the lyrics to the famous hymn "I Am a Child of God" originally read, "Teach me all that I must *know* to live with Him someday"? President Spencer W. Kimball requested that the words be changed to "Teach me all that I must *do* to live with Him someday."[9]

Consider singing "I Am a Child a God" as a closing hymn at your next family home evening, and ponder how the change in the lyrics could spark a change in your own life.

Teach the Plan!

The "Big Picture" of the Plan of Salvation

Objective: To help learners gain a clear understanding of the "big picture" of the plan of salvation.

Attention Getter: Show your children a map of the Amazon rain forest or the Sahara desert. Ask your children the question next to Teach the Plan #1.

Question: Ask your children the question next to Teach the Plan #2 and have a child read the accompanying quote from President Boyd K. Packer.

Visual: Watch the video linked at Teach the Plan #3.

Activity: Give each of your children a blank piece of paper and something to draw with. Invite each child to draw out the major parts of the plan of salvation. Then show them the different depictions of the plan of salvation that follows Teach the Plan #4.

Discussion Questions: The following questions may help your children in understanding, identifying, and applying some gospel truths related to the plan of salvation:

Teach the Plan #5: "What do you think are the strengths and weaknesses of each of these illustrations of the plan of salvation? How do they help us better understand the plan of salvation?"

Teach the Plan #6: "How would you summarize the plan of salvation using five words or less?"

Activity: Give your children a game that they don't know how to play. Tell them to start playing. When they make a move say, "No, you can't do that," but don't tell them why or why not. When they become frustrated at not knowing the rules or understanding the point of the game, compare the game to our mortal life. Ask "How is this like what happens when you don't understand the plan of salvation?"

Invitation to Act: Review the quotes by Joseph Smith and Elder Bruce R. McConkie near the Experiment upon the Word icon. Invite your children to ponder on how learning more about the plan of salvation can affect their daily actions and their personal happiness. Have them choose a chapter in this book that they will commit to study and apply its content.

Act I

Before We
Came to Earth

1

Our First Childhood

Quick quiz! Don't panic—it's just true or false.

1. True or False: God is the father of the spirits of all mankind.

2. True or False: We had agency (the ability to choose) in the premortal existence.

3. True or False: Gender was an essential characteristic of who we were in the premortal existence.

4. True or False: There was no sin in the premortal existence.

5. True or False: Some people, like Cain or Judas, were foreordained in the premortal existence to do evil on earth.

(Note: The answers to this quiz are on page 18).

These next questions are a little tougher. Ready?

- "Where did I come from?"
- "Why I am here?"
- "Where am I going?"

These are three key questions about life that everybody needs answered. Throughout this book, we will address each one of those questions. This chapter will give some answers to the first one: where we came from. President Joseph F. Smith taught, "Where did we come from? From God. Our spirits existed before they came to this world. They were in the councils of the heavens before the foundations of the earth were laid. We were there. We sang together with the heavenly hosts for joy when the foundations of the earth were laid, and when the plan of our existence upon this earth and redemption were mapped out. We were there."[1]

Can you remember what the premortal existence was like? We're guessing that you probably can't because of something called "the veil." The veil makes it so that we cannot remember the things that happened before we were born on earth. But just as surely as we live now, we each lived then.

Our premortal existence lasted a long time—much, much longer than the mortal life we are now experiencing. Everyone on this earth actually lived for a very long time before they were ever born on earth. So, who were we in the premortal existence, and what did we do for all those uncountable years before we came to earth?

We Were Born and Raised as Spirit Children of Heavenly Parents

First of all, each of us was born and raised as a spirit child of Heavenly Parents. Each of us is literally a child of God, created, raised, and reared by our loving Heavenly Father and Heavenly Mother in the premortal existence. Speaking to the prophet Jeremiah, the Lord said, "Before I formed thee in the belly I knew thee" (Jeremiah 1:5). Each of us, like Jeremiah, was known by God before we were born. In fact, President Ezra Taft Benson said, "Nothing is going to startle us more when we pass through the veil to the other side than to realize how well we know our Father and how familiar his face is to us."[2]

We sometimes forget we are eternal beings, the spirit offspring of God. As a son or daughter of a Heavenly King, we are each a prince or a princess. (Perhaps that's why we love fairy tales so much! Deep down inside of our spirits, we all know we are royalty.) As God's children, all of mankind has the potential to be "heirs of God" (Romans 8:17). We were born of Greatness, and for greatness.

 Scan this QR code or visit http://www .youtube.com/watch?v=wiiadnMvm20 to learn more about your true identity.

We Progressed Spiritually

One of the purposes of the premortal existence was to teach us about God's plan and to develop our spiritual capacities. Just as we can grow and develop spiritually in our mortal lifetime, we progressed spiritually in many ways during our premortal existence. *True to the Faith* teaches, "Throughout your premortal life, you developed your identity and increased your spiritual capabilities. Blessed with the gift of agency, you made important decisions, such as the decision to follow Heavenly Father's plan. These decisions affected your life then and now. You grew in intelligence and learned to love the truth, and you prepared to come to the earth, where you could continue to progress."[3]

Speaking of "choice spirits who were reserved to come forth in the fulness of times" (people like you!), the Doctrine and Covenants states, "Even before they were born, they, with many others, received their first lessons in the world of spirits and were prepared to come forth in the due time of the Lord to labor in his vineyard for the salvation of the souls of men" (Doctrine and Covenants 138:53, 56). Based upon our agency and level of obedience to God's laws, some increased more than others in spiritual knowledge, intelligence, and ability.[4] As a result of how we developed, our Heavenly Father foreordained us to specific missions and responsibilities that needed to be performed here on earth. (See chapter 4 for more on fore-ordination.)

We Developed Talents and Abilities

Most of us have a talent that we are naturally good at or an aptitude to which we seem inherently inclined. That could have come through our DNA, but it also could have come from our PMA (premortal abilities)! Elder Bruce R. McConkie wrote:

> Being subject to law, and having their agency, all the spirits of men, while yet in the Eternal Presence [or premortal existence], developed aptitudes, talents, capacities, and abilities of every sort, kind, and degree. During the long expanse of life which then was, an infinite variety of talents and abilities came into being. As the ages rolled, no two spirits remained alike. Mozart became a musician; Einstein centered his interest in mathematics: Michelangelo turned his attention to painting. Cain was a liar, a schemer, a rebel who maintained a close affinity to Lucifer. Abraham and Moses and all of the prophets sought and obtained the talent for spirituality. . . . The whole house of Israel, known and segregated out from their fellows, was inclined toward spiritual things. . . .
>
> . . . When we pass from preexistence to mortality, we bring with us the traits and talents there developed.[5]

Some of what we are doing on earth now is putting the talents and abilities we developed in the premortal existence to use. *For the Strength of Youth* teaches us that we are "responsible for developing the talents and abilities Heavenly Father has given [us]."[6]

We Fought in the "War in Heaven"

For those who are more prone to say, "I'm a lover, not a fighter," well, actually, in the premortal existence you loved God so much you decided to be a fighter. One of the most important events that happened in the premortal existence was what is commonly known as the War in Heaven (Revelation 12:7). (See chapter 3 for more on the War in Heaven.)

We Looked Forward to Earth Life with Excitement

What has been the greatest moment of your life? When you won the state championship? When you went on your first date? When you were chosen as the lead in the school play? When you finally found that missing sock? (Hallelujah!) All great moments to be sure, but not the greatest of your life. In fact, we have forgotten one of our greatest moments.

Elder Richard G. Scott taught: "One of the most exhilarating moments of your life—when you were filled with anticipation, excitement, and gratitude—you are not able to remember. That experience occurred in the premortal life when you were informed that finally your time had come to leave the spirit world to dwell on earth with a mortal body. You knew you could learn through personal experience the lessons that would bring happiness on earth, lessons that would eventually lead you to exaltation and eternal life as a glorified, celestial being in the presence of your Holy Father and His Beloved Son. . . . Oh, how you must have rejoiced with that prospect."[7]

The scriptures teach us that in the premortal existence we "sang together" and "shouted for joy" (Job 38:7) about our opportunity to come to earth and advance in the plan of salvation. We knew that mortal life wouldn't be easy, but we looked forward to it.

President Spencer W. Kimball taught, "We understood well before we came to [earth] that there would be sorrows, disappointments, hard work, blood, sweat, and tears; but in spite of all, we looked down and saw this earth being made ready for us, and we said in effect, 'Yes, Father, in spite of all those things I can see great blessings that could come to me as one of thy sons or daughters; in taking a body I can see that I will eventually become immortal like thee, that I might overcome the effects of sin and be perfected, and so I am anxious to go to the earth at the first opportunity.' And so we came."[8]

For thousands of years, God prepared us in the premortal existence to come here and to succeed in His plan of salvation. And we were excited to be born and have the opportunity to prove ourselves to Him and progress to become more like Him.

Don't Drop the Baton!

In the 2008 Olympics, both the American men's 4x100 meter relay team and the women's team faced the same challenge: as the baton was passed from one runner to the next, a mistake was made and the baton was dropped. Because of this error, both American teams were disqualified.

 Scan this QR code or visit http://delivr .com/1k78r to watch the women's 4x100 meter relay race from the 2008 Olympics.

In a way we can consider life (from its eternal perspective) as a sort of relay race, only in this race we pass the baton to ourselves. We ran the first leg of the race in the premortal existence and successfully finished that portion of the test. We then passed the baton to ourselves here in mortality. We've all succeeded in the first part of the race. Let's not drop the baton as we get ready to pass into the third and final leg of the race, immortality!

Have your own relay race where you practice passing a baton from one person to another. What makes for a successful handoff? How is this like the transition from our living in the premortal existence to our mortal life? How is it different?

One of the best things we can do to act on the truth of the premortal existence is to study the scriptures. Go to the Topical Guide and look up "Man, Antemortal Existence of." The verses listed all describe the premortal existence. Look up the verses and mark the ones that are most meaningful to you.

Still Have Questions?

Could we sin in the premortal existence?

Alma 13:3 teaches that in the premortal existence we were "left to choose good or evil" (Alma 13:3). We each had our agency, and could therefore choose to follow God's instructions, or to not. Doctrine and Covenants 93:38 says, "Every spirit of man was innocent in the beginning; and God having redeemed man from the fall, men became *again,* in their infant state, innocent before God" (emphasis added). So when we began our premortal existence, we were all innocent. Notice that this verse says that when we were infants, we became innocent *again,* thus implying we weren't still innocent and had made some mistakes before we were born. This seems logical considering that a third part of God's children decided to not follow God and instead chose to follow Satan (Doctrine and Covenants 29:36).

Answers to the quiz from page 11

1. True. Acts 17:29; Romans 8:16.
2. True. Doctrine and Covenants 29:36.
3. True. "Gender is an essential characteristic of individual premortal, mortal, and eternal identity and purpose."[9]
4. False. A third part of Heavenly Father's children rebelled against God and His plan (Doctrine and Covenants 29:36; Moses 4:3).
5. False. "No person was foreordained or appointed to sin or to perform a mission of evil. . . . Cain was promised by the Lord that if he would do well, he would be accepted. Judas had his agency."[10]

Teach the Plan!

Our First Childhood

Objective: To help learners understand and appreciate the premortal existence and how it relates to their lives.

Attention Getter: Take the true or false quiz next to Teach the Plan #1.

Quotation: Read the quote by President Joseph F. Smith under Teach the Plan #2. Ask your children, "How does it affect your life to realize that you lived with God before you were born?"

Discussion Question: Discuss the text next to Teach the Plan #3, then ask your children: "What does it mean to you to know that you are born for greatness? How should that affect how you live?"

Video: Watch the video linked at Teach the Plan #4.

Discussion Question: After reading the quote by Elder Bruce R. McConkie next to Teach the Plan #5, ask your children, "What talents and traits do you think you brought to earth from the premortal existence?"

Video: Teach the Plan #6: Watch the video of the failed baton exchange at the Olympics and discuss the associated story.

Activity: Experiment upon the Word: Have a baton relay race, then ask the questions that accompany the activity.

Invitation to Act: Invite your children to act on the challenge offered at Live the Plan. A few days later, follow up with them on their study and invite them to share the verses they studied and marked.

2

The Creation of Our World

"In the beginning God created the heaven and the earth" (Genesis 1:1).

These ten words written by Moses form the foundational account of the creation of this world. These ten words teach us that this universe did not come about by random chance or accident. These ten words teach us that God controlled the events that took place, and that this world has a definite purpose.

What was the purpose of the creation of this earth? The Lord tells us:

> For mine own purpose have I made these things. . . .
> And by the word of my power, have I created them. . . .
> For behold, this is my work and my glory—to bring to pass
> the immortality and eternal life of man. (Moses 1:31–32, 39)

How Was It Done?

Sometimes we have students ask us, "But if God created the world, then what about the Big Bang theory?"

Well, what about it? If God wanted to cause a big bang, or a little boom, it doesn't matter. *How* God created this world is not as important as the reasons *why* He created it, nor does it diminish the truth that God oversaw the formation of this world.

God is the supreme creator of this world. By Him the entire

universe—both large and small—was planned, formed, and began to function. Elder Richard G. Scott taught:

> If we were capable of moving outward into space, we would first see our earth as did the astronauts. Farther out, we would have a grandstand view of the sun and its orbiting planets. They would appear as a small circle of objects within an enormous panorama of glittering stars. Were we to continue the outward journey, we would have a celestial view of our Milky Way spiral, with over 100 billion stars rotating in a circular path, their orbits controlled by gravity around a concentrated central region. Beyond that, we could look toward a group of galaxies called the Virgo Cluster, which some feel includes our Milky Way, estimated to be about 50 million light years away. Beyond that, we'd encounter galaxies 10 billion light years away that the Hubble telescope has photographed. The dizzying enormity of that distance is suggested by noting that light travels 700 million miles an hour. Even from this extraordinary perspective there would not be the slightest evidence of approaching any limit to God the Father's creations.
>
> As awe inspiring as this incredible view of the heavens would present, there is another consideration equally capable of confirming the unfathomable capacities of our Father in Heaven. Were we to move in the opposite direction to explore the structure of matter, we could get a close-up view of a double helix molecule of DNA. That is the extraordinary, self-duplicating molecular structure that controls the makeup of our physical body. Further exploration would bring us to the level of an atom, composed of the protons, neutrons, and electrons we've heard about.[1]

The prophet Alma said, "All things denote there is a God; yea, even the earth, and all things that are upon the face of it, yea, and its motion, yea, and also all the planets which move in their regular form do witness that there is a Supreme Creator" (Alma 30:44). As we look at the grandness and complexities of our earth and the universe, it testifies there is a Great Creator.

An Ordered Creation

We learn from the scriptures that under the direction of His Father, Jesus Christ created the earth and everything on it (see Colossians 1:16). To give an analogy, God the Father could be seen as the chief architect and Christ as the master builder in the creation of this world. We also know from the scriptures the order in which things were created on this earth—from forming the earth, to light appearing, to land appearing, to grasses to water creatures and birds to land animals to people.

In some scriptures these are called the six "days" of creation (see Genesis 1; Moses 2), but the account of the creation in the book of Abraham suggests that the *order* of the Creation is more important than the amount of *time* it took to create the world. In the book of Abraham, the creative "days" are called creative "times" (see Abraham 4), or creative periods. We don't know how long these creative "times" or periods took, so don't freak out on your science teacher if he or she tells you it took billions of years to create the earth. The creative periods might have taken that long.

An Organized Creation

The scriptures also teach that God did not just create everything out of nothing—the earth was organized from existing elements or materials. "And they went down at the beginning, and they, that is the Gods, *organized* and formed the heavens and the earth" (Abraham 4:1; emphasis added).

 Take a look at the following letters and organize them into as many words as possible.

ADESHOPILR

How many did you find?

Just like how you organized those random letters into organized and meaningful words, God took random matter and organized it into meaningful *worlds*, like ours. The scriptures teach the truth that "the elements are eternal" (Doctrine and Covenants 93:33), and by taking unorganized elements that already existed, God organized this world. Thus, according to the Prophet Joseph Smith, technically "the word created [in the scriptures] should be formed, or organized."[2]

And how many worlds were created? The scriptures teach us that God's creations are "as the sand of the sea, which cannot be measured nor numbered" (Hosea 1:10) and that "there is no end to [God's] works" of creation (Moses 1:38). Take a very small pinch of sand—if you don't have any sand handy, use salt instead. Try to count the number of grains in that tiny amount.

A Spiritual Creation

It is also interesting to know that when God created the earth He created everything twice—first spiritually and then physically. In Moses 3:5 we read, "For I, the Lord God, created all things, of which I have spoken, spiritually, before they were naturally upon the face of the earth."

In other words, before the animals or plants were put on earth they were spiritually created. Before humans were made physically we were created spiritually.

What Does the Creation of the World Mean to Me?

Each of these truths—who created the earth, why it was created, and how it was planned and organized—teach us many things about ourselves. Let's take a look at a few lessons we learn from the creation:

Mankind Is God's Crowning Creation

The creation account teaches us that mankind is God's crowning creation. Only after God formed this earth, created light, caused land to appear in the midst of water, and created vegetation and animal life—only then did "God [create] man in his own image" (Genesis 1:27). After each stage of creation God said "that it was good" (Genesis 1:4, 10, 12, 18, 21, 25) but only when mankind—His ultimate creation—was placed on the earth, only then did God say that "it was very good" (Genesis 1:31).

The truth that we are created in the image of God teaches us that our physical bodies are something to be treated with respect, taken care of, and not to be defiled in any way. Paul taught the Corinthians, "Your body is the temple of the Holy Ghost which is in you, which ye have of God" (1 Corinthians 6:19). God has given us our bodies as sacred gifts, and we should treat them as such. The divinity of our physical creation informs many of the commandments related to the body, including obeying the Word of Wisdom, dressing modestly, being sexually pure, and not tattooing or piercing our bodies. By obeying these commandments related to the body, "you can show that you know how precious your body is."[3]

"It Is Not Good That the Man Should Be Alone"

God created males and females because "it is not good that the man should be alone" (Genesis 2:18). God also knew that without each other, men and women could never become exalted. (See chapter 6.)

The creation of the world teaches us a fundamental truth: Man is made for woman, and woman is made for man, and "neither is the man without the woman, neither the woman without the man, in the Lord" (1 Corinthians 11:11). In our world that sometimes confuses the roles of men and women, that sometimes presents and promotes alternative relationships as acceptable, or that sometimes tries to say that being single is somehow more fun and enjoyable than being married and having a family, we should remember the eternal truth clarified and declared from the creation that it is not good for man to be alone.

The fundamental purpose of creation is centered in creating eternal marriages and families: "Wherefore, it is lawful that [a man] should have one wife, and they twain shall be one flesh, and all this that the earth might answer the end of its creation" (Doctrine and Covenants 49:16).

The Earth Was Created for Man—and We Are Stewards over the Earth's Resources

God created the earth for mankind. The Lord said, "For, behold, the beasts of the field and the fowls of the air, and that which cometh of the earth, is ordained for the use of man for food and for raiment, and that he might have in abundance" (Doctrine and Covenants 49:19). However, this gift of the earth should be treated with care. It is our responsibility to take care of the earth and use its resources "with prudence and thanksgiving" (Doctrine and Covenants 89:11). This doesn't mean that we have to stop using electricity, but there are lots of simple things that we can do to protect the earth and be more responsible with God's creations.

When we really understand the gift of the creation, we will be inspired to do simple things to protect the earth.

We Can Follow Patterns from the Creation in Our Lives

There are many things that God did in the creation that we can adapt and adopt in our personal lives. The creation account teaches us how God used one day to prepare for an upcoming day. Check this out:

Day 1: Separates light from darkness

Day 2: Separates waters (firmament)

Day 3: Dry land appears—grass, trees, fruit, etc.

Day 4: Creates the sun, moon, and stars to give light

Day 5: Creates water animals and fowls

Day 6: Creates land animals and mankind

Do you see how the actions in column one made it possible for the Lord to accomplish the actions in column two? Day four couldn't have happened without day one, and day five without day two, and day six without day three. Similarly, the groundwork we lay in our life now it makes it possible for us to accomplish our goals later in life. The groundwork of faith, obedience, and testimony makes it possible to later create missions, temple marriage, and family in our life. As we lay the foundation of attending class, studying, and getting good grades, we will be able to create our dreams of going to college or getting into our chosen career. What we do *today* creates what we can make *tomorrow*.

 Here are some other simple, powerful truths we can apply from the creation:

- "God said, Let there be lights in the firmament of the heaven to divide the day from the night" (Genesis 1:14). Just as God divided the light from the darkness, we can divide truth and error in our lives. We can conclusively draw lines between what is right and what is wrong, and we can make up our minds to choose the right through the light that God has given us in scriptures, the words of the prophets, and by the Holy Ghost.

- God created grass, trees, rivers, mountains, and animals. He gave us a wide variety of things to appreciate. Similarly, we can enhance our lives by making sure that we are involved in a variety of different activities—not just watching TV or being glued to the computer 24/7. Being willing to learn new skills, meet new people, go to new places, and add righteous variety to our lives helps us be more well-rounded people.

- Just as God created all things spiritually before creating them physically, we can set goals and make plans for the things we hope to accomplish and create in the future. President Howard W. Hunter taught: "We must have positive and definite goals in mind. Success in life, school, marriage, business, or any other pursuit doesn't come by accident, but as the result of a well-defined plan and a concentrated effort to bring about a realization of the plan."[4]

- As part of the creation process, God "organized" matter; we can become better organized as well (see Abraham 4:12). Let us organize our folders, our planners, our schedules, our lockers, our cars, and our bedrooms. God is a God of order, and so we should have order in our lives as well (see Doctrine and Covenants 88:119).

- The scriptures teach us that "on the seventh day God ended his work which he had made; and he rested on the seventh day from all his work. . . . And God blessed the seventh day, and sanctified it" (Genesis 2:2–3). Similarly, as we rest from our work in order to worship God on the Sabbath, we will find peace, rejuvenation, and spiritual strength for the upcoming week. If our Creator took a day to rest and made it holy, His creations should too.

We Can Be Creators

Think about this: God is the master creator, and we are supposed to become like Him. So if He is a creator, we should create things too. Several prophets have taught this principle by word and example. Nephi said, "I did teach my people to build buildings, and to work in all manner of wood, and of iron, and of copper, and of brass, and of steel, and of gold, and of silver, and of precious ores" (2 Nephi 5:15). In other words, he not only told his people to make stuff—to build things—he showed them how to create. Then he said they lived "after the manner of happiness" (2 Nephi 5:27). Why would creating things make us happy?

President Dieter F. Uchtdorf offered one answer:

> Creating and being compassionate are two objectives that contribute to our Heavenly Father's perfect happiness. . . .
>
> The desire to create is one of the deepest yearnings of the human soul. No matter our talents, education, backgrounds, or abilities, we each have an inherent wish to create something that did not exist before.
>
> Everyone can create.[5]

There is an inherent joy in making something out of nothing. We can create a painting, a piece of music, or put pen to paper and write. We can make furniture, make scrapbooks, make gardens, or make a meal. We can create laughter, create parties, or create memories. On the most divine level, we can create eternal marriages and families. We can all make something with the gifts and opportunities we have, and doing so will contribute to our happiness.

Scan this QR code or visit http://www .youtube.com/watch?v=RhLlnq5yY7k to see a video of President Dieter F. Uchtdorf talking about the power of creation.

Just as God is a creator, *you* can be a creator too. Sometime in the next week create something—it could be a cooking creation, a drawing, a musical piece—anything. Even if you don't think you're very talented, remember what President Uchtdorf said: "Everyone can create." Take enough time to do it right, and feel the joy that comes from being a creator.

The Creation Helps Us Feel God's Love

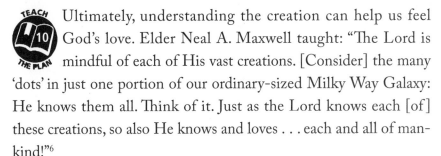 Ultimately, understanding the creation can help us feel God's love. Elder Neal A. Maxwell taught: "The Lord is mindful of each of His vast creations. [Consider] the many 'dots' in just one portion of our ordinary-sized Milky Way Galaxy: He knows them all. Think of it. Just as the Lord knows each [of] these creations, so also He knows and loves . . . each and all of mankind!"[6]

Take a look at this scripture chain that teaches this principle:

- Moses 1:33–35: "Worlds without number [God has] created . . . and innumerable are they unto man; but all things are numbered unto me, for they are mine and I know them."
- Alma 26:37: "We see that God is mindful of every people, whatsoever land they may be in; yea, he numbereth his people, and his bowels of mercy are over all the earth."
- Mosiah 27:30: "He remembereth every creature of his creating."
- Matthew 10:30: "But the very hairs of your head are all numbered."

In the midst of His worlds without end, God numbers, remembers, cares for, and watches over each individual on this earth—the very hairs of our head—because He loves us. The creation teaches us that, and much, much more.

Accidental Creation?

Some people say the creation of the world was an accident, but there is no way that it just *happened*. That would be like having millions of letters accidentally rearranging themselves into the dictionary.

Still not convinced? Try this experiment:

Get a jigsaw puzzle with at least a hundred pieces. Keep all the pieces in the box. Now shake the box seven times. Open the box. Are all the pieces in all the right places? No? Try again. And again. You could do this a thousand times and do you know what? The pieces would never all be in the right place.

Now think of all the millions of cells in your body. Did they all fall into the right place by chance? No way!

Or try this experiment: Take ten small paper squares and number them one through ten. Put them inside an envelope and mix them up really well. Without looking, see if you can pull out the number one from the envelope on the first try. (The odds are 1 in 10.)

Put the number back in the envelope and mix up the numbers again. See if you can be lucky enough to pull out number one and then number two in successive order. (The odds are 1 in 90.) What are the odds that someone could pull out all ten numbers in sequential order? About 1 in 3 million.

There *is* a great creator. If the earth's axis, or its proximity to the sun, or thousands of other minute details about our planet were slightly different, life would not exist on this planet. The same holds true for our bodies and all of creation. Those who have ever created anything in their life know that sublime creations do not happen by chance, but are carefully orchestrated by a creator.

Still Have Questions?

What does the creation teach us about women?

 President Gordon B. Hinckley taught a powerful truth that helps us understand what the creation teaches about women. He said,

Woman is God's supreme creation. Only after the earth had been formed, after the day had been separated from the night, after the waters had been divided from the land, after vegetation and animal life had been created, and after man had been placed on the earth, was woman created; and only then was the work pronounced complete and good.

Of all the creations of the Almighty, there is none more beautiful, none more inspiring than a lovely daughter of God who walks in virtue with an understanding of why she should do so, who honors and respects her body as a thing sacred and divine, who cultivates her mind and constantly enlarges the horizon of her understanding, who nurtures her spirit with everlasting truth.[7]

Some would have us believe that women are second-class citizens, people of lesser importance than men. But the creation teaches us that woman is God's supreme creation.

What does the Church teach about the age of the earth, the theory of evolution, and the origin of man?

Although the Church doesn't have an official stand on evolution, they do have a position on the origin of man. The First Presidency made official statements in 1909 and again in 1925 that officially declared the Church's position. Summarizing these statements, the First Presidency in 1931 said:

Upon the fundamental doctrines of the Church we are all agreed. Our mission is to bear the message of the restored gospel to the world. Leave geology, biology, archaeology, and anthropology, no one of which has to do with the salvation of the souls of mankind, to scientific research, while we magnify our calling in the realm of the Church. . . .

Upon one thing we should all be able to agree, namely, that [The First Presidency in 1909] were right when they said: "Adam is the primal parent of our race."[8]

What does the creation teach us about God and His love for us?

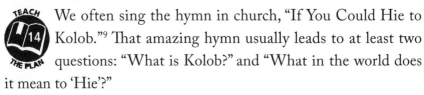 When you put a lot of energy and effort into something, how do you feel about it? You probably really care about it. We are God's greatest creations, and therefore He cares the greatest about us. He cares so much for us that not only did God create what we *need*, He created other things simply to make the world a beautiful place for us to live in. The scriptures teach that "all things . . . are made for the benefit and the use of man, *both to please the eye and to gladden the heart*" (Doctrine and Covenants 59:18; emphasis added). When we look out at a beautiful vista in nature, or see a beautiful animal or other creation, just remember that God made things not only to function, but to be beautiful as well, because He loves us as His greatest creation.

What is Kolob?

We often sing the hymn in church, "If You Could Hie to Kolob."[9] That amazing hymn usually leads to at least two questions: "What is Kolob?" and "What in the world does it mean to 'Hie'?"

Kolob is "the first creation, nearest to the celestial, or the residence of God. First in government, the last pertaining to the measurement of time" (Pearl of Great Price, Facsimile 2:1). One day on Kolob equals "one thousand years according to the [earth's] time" (Abraham 3:4). So, when we sing about hieing to Kolob, we are singing about approaching nearer to the throne of God and understanding His marvelous plan of salvation more completely.

Oh, and to "hie" means to go somewhere fast, or quickly.[10] Use that one next time you've gotta leave: "Hey, guys, lets *hie* outta here." You could be a trendsetter with that one.

Teach the Plan!

The Creation of Our World

Objective: To help learners understand why God created the world, and how the creation is relevant to our lives today.

Attention Getter: Teach the Plan #1: Play a short clip of an inspiring anthem—perhaps the opening to Beethoven's Fifth Symphony or the "Hallelujah" chorus as performed by the Mormon Tabernacle Choir. (Or perhaps even the theme music to *Star Wars*.) As the music plays, read Genesis 1:1 in a loud, dramatic voice.

Discussion Question and Visual: Some people wonder if God created the earth or whether its creation came about through a "Big Bang." If this is a question your children have, share with them the information next to Teach the Plan #2. After reading Elder Richard G. Scott's quote, share some color images of the universe (options are available at http://seek.deseretbook.com/bigpicture).

Lesson Activities: The object lessons next to Teach the Plan #3 and #4 and Experiment upon the Word can be used at different times throughout this lesson to illustrate principles about the Creation. Use any or all of them that you feel might best interest your children and lead into a discussion of truths related to the creation of the world.

Discussion Question: After sharing the principles associated with Teach the Plan #5, ask your children, "How could truly understanding the sacredness of our bodies change the way we treat our bodies?"

Discussion Question: After discussing the principles associated with Teach the Plan #6, ask your family, "What are some things we could do as a family and as individuals to be good stewards of the earth we have been given?"

Lesson Activity: As you share the applications from the Creation next to Teach the Plan #7 remember to include relevant experiences from your life. Ask your children for examples from their lives as well. For example, consider this question: "How has setting goals helped you in your life?"

Discussion Question and Video: After sharing President Dieter F. Uchtdorf's quote from Teach the Plan #8, ask your children, "How has being creative brought you happiness?" Show the video linked at Teach the Plan #9.

Quotation and Discussion Question: Teach the Plan #10: Share the quotation from Elder Neal A. Maxwell and discuss the following question with your children: "What thoughts and feelings do you have knowing that, even though God has created billions of people, He knows and loves you personally?"

Additional Discussion Questions: There are several questions in this chapter that may or may not be relevant to your children (see Teach the Plan #11, #12, #13, and #14). Select those questions that will be of interest to your children and ask your children for their response. As needed, use material from the book to answer the questions.

Invitation to Act: Invite your family members to take the Live the Plan invitation and create something personal and memorable.

3

The War in Heaven

"And there was war in heaven: Michael and his angels fought against the dragon; and the dragon fought and his angels, and prevailed not; neither was their place found any more in heaven. And the great dragon was cast out, that old serpent, called the Devil" (Revelation 12:7–9).

For those who don't think of themselves as much of a warrior or a soldier, think again. You fought in perhaps the greatest war in the history of mankind: one for the very souls of all of God's children. This war took place in the premortal existence before any of us were ever born on earth.

Although we battled in that war, we don't remember it because we have passed from the premortal existence through the veil and into mortality. Fortunately for us, the scriptures and the prophets have helped reveal to us what took place in the War in Heaven so we can better know how to faithfully continue to fight Satan during the war for our souls on earth.

Unfortunately, some people don't read their scriptures carefully enough or often enough, and at times the events of the premortal War in Heaven are not taught or learned in church discussions quite as accurately as they should be. See if you can pick out some of the errors in the following hypothetical summary of the War in Heaven:

In the premortal existence, God the Father wanted to know what He should do, so there were two plans presented: one by Jesus and one by Lucifer (Satan). Satan said that in his plan he wanted everyone to be saved but that to do it he would take away our agency and force us to heaven. Jesus said that in his plan he would save all those who chose righteousness but that some people would be lost because they wouldn't choose to be righteous. We all voted and picked Jesus' plan, and Satan got mad and rebelled and got kicked out of heaven and was sent to outer darkness.

Aside from the fact that there was a premortal existence, not much else in that summary is true. We count *at least* four major things wrong with this statement about the War in Heaven. Knowing what really happened there is essential to know what is really happening here on earth.

Four Important Truths about the War in Heaven

 Here are four things to know and apply from the *real* war which took place in the premortal existence.

There Was Only One Plan—God the Father's Eternal Plan

The War in Heaven was not about a choice between Jesus' plan and Satan's plan. It was a war over *the* plan—the one and only eternal plan of God the Father. God wasn't confused and said, "Who here has a plan?" Jesus didn't come up with the plan—He accepted to be part of God's plan. The family proclamation teaches that in the premortal existence we "knew and worshiped God as [our] Eternal Father and accepted *His* plan by which His children could obtain a physical body and gain earthly experience to progress toward perfection."[1]

President J. Reuben Clark Jr. said that God "is not a novice, he is not an amateur; he has been over this course time and time and time again."[2] The plan of salvation is "one eternal round" (1 Nephi 10:19), and has been and will be "executed and re-executed, again and again," according to what Elder Neal A. Maxwell taught.[3] Thus, as His children we can trust and follow God our Father and His "eternal plan of redemption" (Alma 34:16)—because it was and is the only plan.

Satan's Premortal Plan Was to Serve Himself

In the premortal existence, Satan was originally known as "Lucifer," which means "Light Bringer"[4] or "son of the morning" (Doctrine and Covenants 76:26). But Satan's desire was not to bring light to others. He wanted only the praise and applause of others. He wanted to be in charge. He wanted to take God the Father's place. He demanded of our Heavenly Father, "Give me thine honor" (Moses 4:1), and he wanted to overthrow God so he could rule on a throne in his wicked, self-serving pride (see Isaiah 14:13–14).

Jesus, on the other hand, humbly and selflessly said to our Heavenly Father, "Thy will be done, and the glory be thine forever" (Moses 4:2). Satan was so jealous of Jesus' predetermined appointment by God as our Savior that he eventually threw what amounted to a two-year-old's temper tantrum, pouting, "I am the Only Begotten, worship me" (Moses 1:19).

Because God our Father rejected Satan's self-glorifying motives, Satan began his work of spreading a great lie about what he could and would do. He said, "I will redeem all mankind, that one soul shall not be lost, and surely I will do it" (Moses 4:1). The problem is, he *couldn't* do it. We often hear that Satan proposed to save us all by taking away our agency (our ability to act and choose for ourselves) and forcing us all to heaven. But that is impossible. Agency is a God-given gift (see Moses 7:32) that has and will exist forever (see Doctrine and Covenants 93:30–31), and it cannot forcibly be taken away.

Satan's proposal to "save everyone" was doubly ridiculous because he was lying about his intentions: he didn't want to save anyone else, only himself. He wasn't interested in making other people like God;

he was only interested in using other people so he could become God. That is one reason why the scriptures say that Satan "was a liar from the beginning" (Doctrine and Covenants 93:25). Satan lied about having a real plan, he lied about how he could accomplish a plan, and he lied about his real intentions. (Liar, liar, premortal pants on fire.)

Unfortunately, Satan used his status as "an angel of God who was in authority" (Doctrine and Covenants 76:25) and persuaded other premortal spirits to rebel against God's plan. Because of Satan's silver-tongued lies "many followed after him" (Abraham 3:28) and "a third part of the hosts of heaven turned he away from [God] because of their agency" (Doctrine and Covenants 29:36).

When he rebelled against God, Satan's name was changed, and he was "called the Devil," which comes from the Hebrew word *diabolos,* meaning "slanderer."[5] That is one reason why the scriptures say Satan was "the accuser of our brethren" (Revelation 12:10).

Our Premortal Weapon Wasn't a Ballot, It Was a Testimony

Fortunately, the greater part of God's children—yes, that includes you—saw through Satan's lies and stayed faithful to God's true plan of salvation. To beat the adversary in the premortal War in Heaven, we didn't use spirit punches, premortal machine guns, or cumulonimbus cloud-bombs. We used weapons that were much more powerful and real than that: Faith in and a testimony of the Lord Jesus Christ and His Atonement.

The scriptures teach us that in the premortal existence the faithful "overcame [Satan] by the blood of the Lamb, and by the word of their testimony; and they loved not their lives unto the death" (Revelation 12:11). You have been exercising faith in Jesus Christ since before you were born. In a way, you're not here to *gain* a testimony—you're here to simply *remember* the one you've always had (see Revelation 12:11).

In the premortal existence, we knew Jesus was the chosen heir of God, and that because of His character He was perfectly capable of performing the Atonement. With that knowledge and with our testimony of Jesus, we rejected Satan's pitiful ploy to try to take Jesus' place.

It wasn't with a vote that we overcame Satan, it was with our testimony of God's Beloved Son. Thus, God said that it was "the power of mine Only Begotten [that] caused that [Satan] should be cast down" (Moses 4:3).

The modern prophets have taught us: "Those who followed Heavenly Father and Jesus Christ were permitted to come to the earth to experience mortality and progress toward eternal life."[6] The fact that you were born on this earth shows you stood on Heavenly Father and Jesus' side before you were ever born.

> **LIVE THE PLAN** Your testimony is a powerful weapon for yourself and others to overcome the adversary. You have had a testimony for thousands of years; you just need to remember it and develop it (see Revelations 12:11). A testimony is remembered and increased as you share it with others,[7] so bear your testimony the next opportunity you have to do so, whether at home, with friends, or at church.

The War Rages Today—on Earth

When Satan was cast out of heaven, where did he go? Sometimes people say Satan and his followers were cast to outer darkness. Thanks for playin', but wrong.

Satan and his followers were not cast into outer darkness—not yet anyway. The scriptures teach us that "the great dragon was cast out, that old serpent, called the Devil, and Satan, which deceiveth the whole world: *he was cast out into the earth,* and his angels were cast out with him" (Revelation 12:9; emphasis added). Right now, Satan is on the earth—our earth—and so are the rebellious third part who followed him. The difference is that when Satan and his premortal minions were cast out, they were denied the privilege of receiving a mortal body, so we simply can't see them.

Another possible difference is that Satan knows he has lost; he has failed (see Revelation 12:12; Matthew 8:29). He knows that truth and goodness and Jesus and God our Father will triumph, and that eventually Satan will be sent "down to the gulf of misery and endless wo" (Helaman 5:12) in outer darkness where he will weep, and wail, and try to gnash his nonexistent teeth (see Alma 40:13). Until then, Satan continues to try "to deceive and to blind men, and to lead them captive at his will" (Moses 4:4). Like a reeling boxer who has been knocked silly, Satan is desperately grasping out as he falls to see who he can drag down with him to "be miserable like unto himself" (2 Nephi 2:27).

The premortal war for the souls of mankind in heaven is not over. It has simply spilled onto a new battlefield. Fortunately for us, as Joseph Smith taught, "The devil has no power over us only as we permit him."[8] We have so many weapons of war at our side to beat him again: We have agency. We have a mortal body. We have the Holy Ghost. We have scriptures that teach us eternal truth. We have living prophets to guide the way. We have the Church to provide us eternal ordinances. We have priesthood power to bless our lives. We have families to love and care for us. We have testimony to power our actions.

Above all, we have Jesus the Christ, "who is mighty to save and to cleanse from all unrighteousness" (Alma 7:14) and who will "subdue all enemies under his feet" (Doctrine and Covenants 76:61). The final outcome is certain: God will win, and His plan of successful salvation will work. The only question today is whether we, individually, will continue to follow it, and beat Satan once more. We did it once, we can do it again.

Stare at this image without blinking for one solid minute. Then, look at a blank white wall or paper and blink rapidly. You will see an image of a face appear. Go on, try it.

Did you notice what happened after ten or twenty seconds? The image started to fade away as you blinked at the blank white paper. If you want to see the face again, you simply need to refocus on the image and do the activity again.

Similarly, our testimonies of Christ will fade if we don't continually refocus on Him through repentance, scripture study, prayer, partaking of the sacrament, attending the temple, and serving others. The more intently we focus on getting to know the Savior, the more we will see His face and know that He is (see Doctrine and Covenants 93:1).

Living in the Last Days

Church leaders have said some impressive things about those living in the last days:

> "For nearly six thousand years, God has held you in reserve to make your appearance in the final days before the Second Coming. Every previous gospel dispensation has drifted into apostasy, but ours will not. . . . God has saved for the final inning some of his strongest children, who will help bear off the kingdom triumphantly. And that is where you come in, for you are the generation that must be prepared to meet your God. . . . Make no mistake about it—you are a marked generation. There has never been more expected of the faithful in such a short period of time as there is of us."—President Ezra Taft Benson[9]

> "I'd like to make this . . . promise to you. If you are faithful, the day will come when those deserving pioneers whom you rightly praise for having overcome the adversities in their wilderness trek will instead praise you for having made your way successfully through a desert of despair, for having passed through a cultural wilderness and having kept the faith."—Elder Neal A. Maxwell[10]

You are the youth of the latter days. Let us press forward and win the war that started so long ago!

Teach the Plan!

The War in Heaven

Objective: To help learners understand what really happened during the War in Heaven and to identify the weapons that will help us continue to overcome the adversary here on earth.

Attention Getter: Teach the Plan #1: To start, ask your children if they can name the first war ever fought in history. After everyone has answered, read Revelation 12:7–9 with them.

Attention Getter: Read the paragraph next to Teach the Plan #2 to your children and see how many errors they can pick out from this summary of the War in Heaven.

Lesson Activity: Have your family explain the four truths outlined under Teach the Plan #3. Go to http://seek.deseretbook.com/bigpicture and download a handout that has each of the four truths on its own page. Give one page to four different people in your family. Let each read the page and then explain what they learned that is different from the hypothetical summary referred to in Teach the Plan #2.

Discussion Questions: The following questions may help your children in understanding, identifying, and applying some gospel truths related to the War in Heaven:

Teach the Plan #4: Why do you think it is important to know that the plan of salvation was given to us by God the Father and not proposed by Jesus Christ?

Teach the Plan #5: Although Satan cannot forcibly take away our agency, in what ways have you seen the adversary try to take away people's ability to choose for themselves? How do the teachings of Jesus Christ help us remain in control of our lives and choices?

Teach the Plan #6: How do you think your personal testimony can help you overcome the temptations of the adversary?

Activity: Do the optical illusion activity next to the Experiment on the Word!

Invitation to Act: Invite your family members to take the Live the Plan invitation and bear their testimony at the next available opportunity.

4

Foreordained for Greatness

 This experiment will teach you about what foreordination is—and is not. Get a pillow and throw it at someone. (Not hard; you don't want to hurt them.) Don't do anything else until you've thrown that pillow.

Did you throw the pillow? If you did, did we "force" you to do it because you were "destined" to? Obviously not. You are free to choose your actions, and you aren't forced by destiny to do anything. Foreordination doesn't mean we are forced to do something; it is more like fulfilling agreements we made in the premortal existence to do specific things.

In *True to the Faith*, we read, "In the premortal spirit world, God appointed certain spirits to fulfill specific missions during their mortal lives. *This is called foreordination*."[1] Although we often read about foreordained Church leaders (see Abraham 3:22–23; Jeremiah 1:5; Doctrine and Covenants 138:55–56), foreordination isn't just for prophets. Many of us seemingly normal, everyday people were also foreordained to do a variety of things in this life.

We Were Foreordained to Be Born at a Specific Time

Among other things that we were foreordained to do, we were foreordained to come to earth when we did. President Ezra Taft Benson said, "You have been born at this time for a sacred and glorious purpose. It is not by chance that you have been reserved to come to earth in this last dispensation of the fulness of times. Your birth at this particular time was foreordained in the eternities."[2]

This truth should motivate us to do our very best to accomplish the things that God sent us here to do. One of Satan's greatest temptations today is to distract us with things that are fun and amusing, but not really that important. However, we weren't saved for the latter days just so that we could be the blessed generation that gets to play Angry Birds.

The truth that we were reserved to be born in the last days should also help us avoid the mentality of "it's so much harder to be righteous today than ever before" that can sometimes creep in and weaken us (see Helaman 13:25). God knew we could handle our day, with its various trials and temptations, just like He knew the faithful Israelites could inherit the promised land and just like He knew Joseph Smith and the early Church leaders could establish the restored Church. Those of us Church members who have come to earth in these latter days were specifically sent here to help "build the kingdom of God and prepare the world for the Second Coming of the Savior."[3]

We Were Foreordained to Accomplish Specific Tasks

Using His foreknowledge, God assigned His children to accomplish certain tasks. For example, we know that Joseph Smith was foreordained to bring forth the Book of Mormon and restore The Church of Jesus Christ of Latter-day Saints (see 2 Nephi 3:12–15).

The scriptures teach us that other individuals were also chosen to accomplish important works on earth. We know that the Founding Fathers of our country (perhaps men like George Washington, John Adams, Thomas Jefferson, and James Madison) were pre-selected to do their great work of founding the United States of America and were "raised up unto this very purpose" (Doctrine and Covenants 101:80).

All young men in the Church who hold the priesthood were foreordained to share the gospel. Joseph Smith taught, "Every man who has a calling to minister to the inhabitants of the world was ordained to that very purpose in the Grand Council of heaven before this world was."[4]

And Elder David A. Bednar said, "Every man who holds the priesthood was foreordained to that very responsibility in the premortal existence. Does a young man who understands that doctrine have a choice to go on a mission? He made that choice before he was ever born."[5]

Being chosen by God in the premortal existence to accomplish specific tasks applies equally to women. Elder Neal A. Maxwell taught, "Just as certain men were foreordained from before the foundations of the world, so were certain women appointed to certain tasks."[6] For example, we know that Mary was designated by God to be the mortal mother of Jesus (see Mosiah 3:8; Alma 7:10).

In 2001, Sheri Dew, second counselor in the general Relief Society presidency, taught in general conference, "Just as worthy men were foreordained to hold the priesthood in mortality, righteous women were endowed premortally with the privilege of motherhood."[7]

It is possible that each of us were asked by God, based on our premortal dispositions and abilities, to fulfill many other specific assignments while we are here on earth that will bless the lives of others.

We Were Foreordained to Develop Christlike Attributes

In a broad sense, all of God's children were foreordained to gain and develop Christlike attributes when we came to earth. President Joseph F. Smith taught, "Christ is the great example for all mankind, and I believe that mankind were as much foreordained to become like him, as that he was foreordained to be the Redeemer of man. . . . We are . . . in the form of God, physically, and may become like him spiritually, and like him in the possession of knowledge, intelligence, wisdom and power."[8]

We have been commanded to develop a Christlike character (see 3 Nephi 12:48; 27:27), and we fulfill our mortal missions as we do so, changing our very natures through Jesus' Atonement and "becoming humble, meek, submissive, patient, full of love and all long-suffering" (Alma 13:28; see also Mosiah 3:19; Doctrine and Covenants 4).

Foreordination Is Not a Guarantee

Just because we were foreordained to something doesn't mean it will happen. In *True to the Faith*, we read, "Foreordination does not guarantee that individuals will receive certain callings or responsibilities. Such opportunities come in this life as a result of the righteous exercise of agency, just as foreordination came as a result of righteousness in the premortal existence."[9]

We each have important missions to fulfill, but if we make wrong choices, we may miss opportunities to accomplish the work we were sent here to perform. Only by keeping the commandments will we be able to accomplish what we were foreordained to do.

Read your patriarchal blessing and look for things that you have been foreordained to do. For example, it might mention callings (such as missionary, father, or mother) that you were given before coming to earth. Even if the word "foreordain" isn't used, your patriarchal blessing can refer to things (like a mission) that you were foreordained to do. Keep in mind that even if your patriarchal blessing doesn't mention specific events (like getting married or having children) that doesn't mean that those things won't happen.

Still Have Questions?

What is the difference between foreordination and predestination?

Predestination is the belief that people are destined to do certain things and that they have no choice in the matter. *Predestination is a false doctrine.* President Brigham Young explained, "God has decreed and foreordained many things that have come to pass, and he will continue to do so; but when he decrees great blessings upon a nation or upon an individual they are decreed upon certain conditions."[10]

For example, if a person's patriarchal blessing says he or she will marry in the temple, that does *not* mean that the person has lost any agency and *must* be married in the temple. It could mean that the person has been foreordained by the Lord to receive the blessing of temple marriage. If the person lives righteously and exercises agency appropriately, then the promised blessing will come to pass.

Were we foreordained to come to specific parents or to marry a specific person?

The Church has not given any official statements on whether or not we knew our earthly parents or siblings in the premortal existence. While it would be nice to think that we knew our families before coming to earth, President Joseph Fielding Smith said, "We have no scriptural justification . . . for the belief that we had the privilege of choosing our parents and our life companions in the spirit world. . . . It is possible that in some instances it is true, but it would require too great a stretch of the imagination to believe it to be so in all, or even in the majority of cases. Most likely we came where those in authority decided to send us."[11]

Teach the Plan!

Foreordained for Greatness

Objective: To help learners understand the doctrine of foreordination and how this doctrine can influence their lives.

Attention Getter: Modify the Experiment upon the Word activity by holding a pillow and asking your children if they think you will throw it at one of them. Make it clear that you haven't decided yet if you will actually throw it or not. Ask, "Does God know whether or not I'm going to throw the pillow? Does the fact that He does know take away my agency?"

Throw the pillow (or don't) and explain how this relates to foreordination as defined at Teach the Plan #1.

Lesson Activity: Plan a "Mission Impossible" activity. Give each person in your family an envelope that contains a "mission"—something that the child is assigned to do. Write the following message: "Your mission, should you choose to accept it, is to _____. This message will self-destruct in five seconds." Have the assigned missions be something that a person can do within two to three minutes. (For example: Do twenty-five push-ups. Pick up five things off the floor. Draw a picture of your best friend. Shake everyone's hand in the room.)

Instruct each person to open the envelopes at the exact same time and fulfill their mission in the next three minutes. When they are done, ask them to make comparisons to how this activity is like foreordination. (Possible answers: The assignments were made beforehand. You could choose to do them or not. There was a limited time period to complete them in. Some tasks were more difficult than others.)

Then ask how this activity isn't like foreordination. (Possible answers: The assignments were random. Some activities served no real purpose. You don't find out your life's mission in an envelope.)

Quotation and Discussion Question: Read the quote from Ezra Taft Benson next to Teach the Plan #2. Ask your children, "Why do you think you have been born at this particular time?"

Quotation and Discussion Question: Read the quotes from Joseph Smith

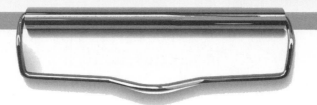

and Elder David A. Bednar next to Teach the Plan #3. Ask your children, "How is a priesthood holder serving a mission an example of foreordination?"

Quotation and Discussion Question: Read the quote from Joseph F. Smith next to Teach the Plan #4. Ask your children, "What could you be doing now to fulfill your foreordained mission to become more like the Savior?"

Quotation and Discussion Question: Read the quote from *True to the Faith* next to Teach the Plan #5. Ask your children, "How can you make sure you fulfill what you were foreordained to do and become?"

Invitation to Act: Invite your family members to take the Live the Plan invitation and read and study their patriarchal blessing. You may need to modify the activity if some family members haven't received their patriarchal blessing.

5

How the Fall of Adam and Eve Affects Us All

Hold your breath. Go on, hold it. See if you can hold it for one minute straight. Ready, go!

Were you able to do it? Actually, we don't care whether you were able to do it or not. What we care about is what you were *thinking* while you were holding your breath. Our guess is that you were probably thinking about breathing—as in "Air. . . . I need air! Breathe! What kind of lame book is this that asks me not to breathe?!"

Now think about this: How many times today had you thought about breathing *before* doing this activity? Probably not even once, as most of us take breathing for granted. But consider this quote from President Ezra Taft Benson:

> Just as a man does not really desire [air] until he [can't breathe], so he does not desire the salvation of Christ until he knows why he needs Christ.
>
> *No one adequately and properly knows why he needs Christ until he understands and accepts the doctrine of the Fall and its effect upon all mankind.*[1]

So what is the Fall of Adam and Eve, and what are its effects on our lives?

Adam and Eve's Garden Dilemma

After God created the earth, Adam and Eve were placed in the Garden of Eden. They "each had a body of flesh and bones that could not die."[2] The scriptures teach that Adam and Eve could have remained in the Garden of Eden forever (see 2 Nephi 2:22). But they couldn't have children in the state they were in, and they didn't know the difference between good and evil (see 2 Nephi 2:23).

While they were in the Garden of Eden, Adam and Eve were "married by the Lord" (Genesis 2, chapter heading). In *Gospel Principles,* we read, "God brought Adam and Eve together in marriage because 'it was not good that the man should be alone' (Moses 3:18)."[3]

Now, here's where things get a little tricky: God gave Adam and Eve two commandments after they were married in the Garden of Eden. First, God told them to, "Be fruitful, and multiply, and replenish the earth" (Moses 2:28). At the same time, God told them they could freely eat of every tree in the garden except one: the tree of knowledge of good and evil. Of that tree God said, "In the day thou eatest thereof thou shalt surely die" (Moses 3:17).

Why were these commandments difficult? Because Adam and Eve couldn't have children unless they were mortal, and they couldn't become mortal unless they ate the forbidden fruit. If they kept the one commandment (no fruit), they couldn't keep the other (have kids). What to do!?

This conundrum has been puzzling to some. But President Joseph Fielding Smith explained, "This is the way I interpret that: The Lord said to Adam, here is the tree of the knowledge of good and evil. If you want to stay here, then you cannot eat of that fruit. If you want to stay here, then I forbid you to eat it. But you may act for yourself, and you may eat of it if you want to. And if you eat it, you will die."[4]

What Happened That Caused Adam and Eve to Fall?

While Adam and Eve were puzzling over their dilemma, along came Lucifer. Lucifer had been cast out from the premortal existence because of his rebellion, and "he became Satan, yea, even the devil, the father of all lies, to deceive and to blind men" (Moses 4:4). He "sought to destroy the world" (Moses 4:6) and the whole plan of salvation, so he tricked Adam and Eve into partaking of the forbidden fruit. But Satan "knew not the mind of God" (Moses 4:6)—meaning he didn't understand that by Adam and Eve partaking of the forbidden fruit the plan of salvation would move forward, not backward!

Satan succeeded in getting Eve to partake of the forbidden fruit. In *Gospel Fundamentals* we read, "When Eve told Adam she had eaten some of the fruit, he knew she would have to leave the garden. He ate some of the fruit, too, so they could stay together."[5] This event (Adam and Eve partaking of the fruit) is what is meant by the Fall.

LIVE THE PLAN Focus on the dot below and move your head forwards and backwards.

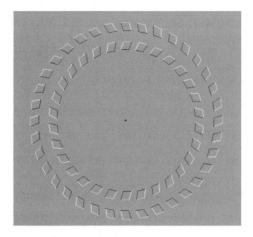

We know those circles aren't *really* moving, but the image is deceiving. Just as Satan designed tricks to deceive Adam and Eve, he is designing tricks to deceive you. We would encourage you to focus on your life and avoid Satan's tricks.

Satan's Tricks

It is interesting to analyze how Satan deceived Adam and Eve. Let's look at four tricks he used on them.

Trick #1: Creating the Illusion of Restrictions

Satan wanted Eve to feel like God was restricting her by saying, "Hath God said—Ye shall not eat of *every* tree of the garden?" (Moses 4:7; emphasis added). We know that the gospel doesn't restrict us, but that living the gospel actually will "make [us] free" (John 8:32).

How does Satan try to get people to sin today by making them think they'll be "more free" if they break commandments?

Trick #2: Downplaying the Consequences

Satan tried to downplay the consequences to Eve of her decision. Eve told Satan that if she ate of the fruit, she would die, and Satan lied, saying, "Ye shall not surely die; for . . . ye shall be as gods, knowing good and evil" (Moses 4:10–11). While it was true that Eve would become able to know good from evil if she ate the fruit, Satan lied and downplayed the consequences.

How does Satan do the same thing today?

Trick #3: Rationalizing and Justifying

Satan tried to get Eve to rationalize and justify that partaking of the forbidden fruit was okay. Notice how she says to herself "that the tree was good for food" and "pleasant to the eyes" and "to be desired to make her wise" (Moses 4:12). Nowhere in this verse does Eve mention that she should partake of the fruit so she can keep the commandment to have children.

How does Satan try to get us to sin by rationalizing and justifying our breaking the commandments?

Trick #4: Hiding the Sin

After Eve partook of the fruit, Adam decided to partake of the forbidden fruit as well. After they did, Satan tried to get them to hide from God for their actions and cover up their transgression. The scriptures say that "Adam and his wife went to hide themselves from the presence of the Lord God" (Moses 4:14).

How does Satan still try to get us to hide our sins from God and cover them up?

What Happened after the Fall?

When Adam and Eve partook of the forbidden fruit, two huge things happened. First, they were cast out of the presence of God in the Garden of Eden. Second, they became mortal. *Gospel Fundamentals* says:

> Our Father in Heaven sent [Adam and Eve] out of the Garden of Eden. They could not walk and talk with him anymore. From then on mankind was separated from the presence of our Father in Heaven. . . .
>
> Their bodies changed. Now they could have children. They could become sick and feel pain and sorrow, and someday they would die. The changes that came upon Adam and Eve are called the fall of Adam.[6]

Although the Fall of Adam and Eve may seem tragic to some, it was actually a great blessing because it moved the plan of salvation forward. *True to the Faith* says that "the Fall is an integral part of Heavenly Father's plan of salvation (see 2 Nephi 2:15–16; 9:6). It has a twofold direction—downward yet forward. In addition to introducing physical and spiritual death, it gave us the opportunity to be born on the earth and to learn and progress."[7]

The scriptures say that Eve was even "glad" about their fallen condition. She said, "Were it not for our transgression we never should have had seed, and never should have known good and evil, and the joy of our redemption, and the eternal life which God giveth unto all the obedient" (Moses 5:11).

What Does the Fall of Adam and Eve Have to Do with Me?

Let's take a look at why Eve was so happy and what the Fall of Adam and Eve has to do with us.

We Get to Be Born and Have a Body

We might not realize it, but *without the fall we would not be here.* Without a body, we could not become like God who has an immortal "body of flesh and bones as tangible as man's" (Doctrine and Covenants 130:22). Elder David A. Bednar taught, "Our physical bodies make possible a breadth, a depth, and an intensity of experience that simply could not be obtained [without a body]."[8] The scriptures teach that our spirits enjoy having a physical body so much that when we are dead and separated from our physical body, we will see "the long absence of [our] spirits from [our] bodies to be a bondage" (Doctrine and Covenants 45:17). So, next time you do something physical, or touch and feel something, or use your physical body in any way that brings joy to your life, thank Adam and Eve for falling.

We Can Use Our Agency

Another blessing of the Fall of Adam and Eve is that, in the words of Adam, our "eyes are opened" (Moses 5:10), and according to Eve, we "have known good and evil" (Moses 5:11). In other words, because of the Fall we have opposition, we know good from evil, and we can use our agency. (See chapter 7.)

Think of living with no opposites, in a boring and neutral world, "having no joy, for [we] knew no misery; doing no good, for [we] knew no sin" (2 Nephi 2:23). Without the fall there would be no "opposition" (2 Nephi 2:15), but, since they did fall, we do have opposition, and therefore we understand opposites.

 For a fun activity, match up the opposites below; it will be good for your body and spirit. (See answers at the bottom of the page.)

Comic	Spurn
Agile	Sharp
Cluster	Arrogant
Assent	Include
Bedlam	Order
Blunt	Refuse
Antique	Awkward
Isolate	Scatter
Humble	Tragic
Desire	Modern

We Inherit a Fallen Nature

But on the bad side, we inherit a fallen nature. Because of the Fall of Adam and Eve, we are born and are mortal—but unfortunately that means we will also die. As a result of the Fall, we can sin and become unclean and unworthy to live with God (see 1 Nephi 15:33–34). Although we don't inherit Adam and Eve's transgression (see Articles of Faith 1:2), we do inherit their fallen condition, and "we are unworthy before [God]; because of the fall our natures have become evil continually" (Ether 3:2). As mortals, we have to battle to overcome the lusts of the flesh like being lazy, selfish, mean, rude, and immoral. The Book of Mormon teaches us that "the natural man

(Answers: Isolate-Include, Desire-Spurn, Humble-Arrogant, Antique-Modern, Blunt-Sharp, Bedlam-Order, Assent-Refuse, Cluster-Scatter, Agile-Awkward, Comic-Tragic)

is an enemy to God, and has been from the fall of Adam" (Mosiah 3:19).

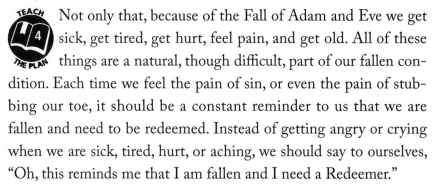Not only that, because of the Fall of Adam and Eve we get sick, get tired, get hurt, feel pain, and get old. All of these things are a natural, though difficult, part of our fallen condition. Each time we feel the pain of sin, or even the pain of stubbing our toe, it should be a constant reminder to us that we are fallen and need to be redeemed. Instead of getting angry or crying when we are sick, tired, hurt, or aching, we should say to ourselves, "Oh, this reminds me that I am fallen and I need a Redeemer."

We Can Be Redeemed

Perhaps the greatest way the Fall of Adam and Eve affects us is that because of spiritual and physical death, Christ covenanted to come to earth to "redeem all mankind" (Moses 4:1). Jesus' Atonement overcomes all of the effects of the Fall of Adam and Eve, and can bring us back to God's presence and help us become like Him. Christ can cleanse us of sin, and rescue and resurrect us from death. (See chapter 8.)

Moroni summarized the entire plan of salvation this way: "Behold, he created Adam, and by Adam came the fall of man. And because of the fall of man came Jesus Christ, even the Father and the Son; and because of Jesus Christ came the redemption of man" (Mormon 9:12). Because of the Fall of Adam and Eve we need a redeemer, and because of Jesus Christ we can be redeemed if we will but come unto Him.

Teach the Plan!

How the Fall of Adam and Eve Affects Us All

Objective: To help learners understand the doctrine of how the Fall affects our mortal life and how the Fall is directly connected to our need to be redeemed through the atonement of Jesus Christ.

Attention Getter: Have your children attempt to hold their breath for one minute. Then read the quote from President Ezra Taft Benson next to Teach the Plan #1.

Visual: Show a visual of Adam and Eve in the Garden of Eden. Ask, "How do you think we can resolve the apparent conflicting commandments to have children but not partake of the forbidden fruit?" After hearing your family's responses, share with them the quote from President Joseph F. Smith next to Teach the Plan #2.

Quotation and Discussion Question: Read the quote from *True to the Faith* next to Teach the Plan #3. Ask your children, "How is the Fall 'downward' and yet still 'forward'?"

Lesson Activity: Do the "opposites" activity next to the Experiment upon the Word icon. Ask your children, "How does the Fall make it so that we have opposites? Why do you think opposites are a necessary part of God's plan?"

Discussion Question: After reading the paragraph next to Teach the Plan #4, ask your children, "How can the small (and large) trials of life remind us of both the Fall and the Atonement?"

Invitation to Act: Do the optical illusion activity next to Live the Plan. Ask your children the questions that go along with the four tricks Satan uses to deceive us today. Invite your children to be on the alert for these tricks and to resist them.

Act II

Life on Earth

6

What Is the Purpose of Our Life?

Perhaps no other questions are asked more often in the hearts and minds of people around the world than "What is the purpose of life?" "What am I doing here?" "What is going on?"

Without the knowledge of the plan of salvation, answering these universal questions about the purpose of life is almost impossible. Even for those who wax philosophical, answers like "The purpose of life is to find purpose" (an answer we really found when doing research for this chapter!) can be more confusing than helpful.

Some people who don't know the gospel plan think that the purpose of life is to be rich, or to be famous, or to be as buff or beautiful as possible. Other people might think the purpose of life is to just have fun. Luckily for us, the Lord restored through Joseph Smith the knowledge of the great plan of salvation, and with that knowledge God restored the answer to the question: What is the purpose of life?

To Become More like God

Some people say that the purpose of life is "to live with God again." Although that can be one of the *benefits* of the plan of salvation, it is not its primary purpose. After all, if the purpose of life were just to live with God, then why did we ever leave the premortal existence in the first place? We are trying to do something more than just *live* with God, we are trying to *become like*

63

Him. As a matter of fact, the entire purpose of life can be summarized in these five simple words: *to become more like God.*

What Is God Like?

If we are here to become more like God, a logical question is "What is God like?" Joseph Smith once said, "I want you all to know [God], and to be familiar with Him."[1] If we don't know or if we have an incorrect idea of what God is like, then it is very difficult to correctly become like Him. That's like trying to dress up like someone for Halloween without knowing what they look like.

For example, if we think that God is a big, giant, floating Spirit, then how do we become like that? Or, if we wrongly think that God is mean and unforgiving, we won't be able to become as He truly is. That is why *Lectures on Faith* says that we must have "a *correct* idea of [God's] character, perfections, and attributes"[2] in order to have faith in God.

The scriptures teach us what our Heavenly Father is *really* like.

- God has an immortal physical body (see Doctrine and Covenants 130:22). When you picture God, please don't picture a floating mass of spirit, or someone who is really old and tired. God is a resurrected, glorified, perfect being! (See chapter 16.)
- God is really smart. Even more than $E=mc^2$ smart. The scriptures teach us that God "knoweth all things, and there is not anything save he knows it" (2 Nephi 9:20).
- God has divine attributes like kindness, love, patience, gentleness, mercy, and empathy (see Alma 26:35; Moroni 8:3).
- God is the father of our spirits (see Romans 8:16). We are children of "heavenly parents."[3]
- God is perfect (see Matthew 5:48).

How does knowing these things about God answer the question about the purpose of life? Because if we are here to become more like God, then knowing about Him tells us what to do and who to become. Based on who God is, the following are five important tasks that help us fulfill our purpose in life:

1. Receive a body and keep it pure.
2. Gain intelligence—light and truth.
3. Develop Godlike attributes.
4. Establish an eternal marriage and family.
5. Come unto Christ and be perfected in Him.

Let's talk about how we can fulfill each of these tasks.

Receive a Body and Keep It Pure

Congratulations! By the mere fact of your birth you have fulfilled one of the fundamental purposes of life—receiving a physical body! So go thank your parents! Actually, you did a lot to gain your body. You were faithful in the premortal existence and in following the Father's plan. (See chapter 3.) If you weren't faithful in the premortal existence, you wouldn't be here!

As a matter of fact, did you know somebody is jealous of your body? The devil is—because he doesn't have one. He wishes he had a body, and he can't stand the fact that we have ours. Because of that jealousy, he tries to get us to misuse our physical bodies and sin.

Elder David A. Bednar taught: "Because a physical body is so central to the Father's plan of happiness and our spiritual development, we should not be surprised that Lucifer seeks to frustrate our progression by tempting us to use our bodies improperly. One of the ultimate ironies of eternity is that the adversary, who is miserable precisely because he has no physical body, invites and entices us to share in his misery through the improper use of our bodies. The very tool he does not have and cannot use is thus the primary target of his attempts to lure us to physical and spiritual destruction."[4]

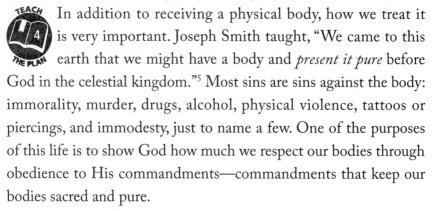 In addition to receiving a physical body, how we treat it is very important. Joseph Smith taught, "We came to this earth that we might have a body and *present it pure* before God in the celestial kingdom."[5] Most sins are sins against the body: immorality, murder, drugs, alcohol, physical violence, tattoos or piercings, and immodesty, just to name a few. One of the purposes of this life is to show God how much we respect our bodies through obedience to His commandments—commandments that keep our bodies sacred and pure.

Gain Intelligence—Light and Truth

As BYU's sign welcoming visitors to their campus proudly proclaims: "The glory of God is intelligence." Doctrine and Covenants 93:36 clarifies, saying, "The glory of God is intelligence, or, in other words, light and truth."

We gain this kind of intelligence "even by study and also by faith" (Doctrine and Covenants 88:118). So our purpose isn't just to learn random facts to answer *Jeopardy!* questions. We aren't fulfilling the plan of salvation if we get an "A" on a test of temples of ancient Egypt, but fail our test of temple recommend questions. We aren't gaining true intelligence by Googling information on the web, and are just "ever learning, and never able to come to the knowledge of the truth" (2 Timothy 3:7). Elder Dallin H. Oaks said that "knowledge is not of equal value. Some knowledge is more important than others. That principle also applies to what we call spiritual knowledge."[6]

Light and truth are only gained through obedience (see Doctrine and Covenants 93:39). Therefore, faithful people who are obedient and full of the Spirit are more "intelligent" than wicked people. Our primary goal regarding gaining intelligence is to gain spiritual knowledge—light and truth.

Of course, light and truth encompass all types of knowledge. Truth is found in science, history, geology, art, and a host of other academic subjects. That is one reason why the Lord commanded us to understand "things both in heaven and in the earth, and under the earth; things which have been, things which are, things which must shortly come to pass; things which are at home, things which are abroad; the wars and the perplexities of the nations" (Doctrine and Covenants 88:79). The modern prophets tell us, "Plan now to obtain an education. Be willing to work diligently and make sacrifices if necessary. . . . Maintain an enthusiasm for learning throughout your life."[7]

After all, we are to become like God, and can you imagine a God who doesn't understand history, science, art, and math? If God understands those subjects, we need to as well. Knowing that God is intelligent is one reason why "education is an important part of Heavenly Father's plan to help you become more like Him."[8]

Elder John A. Widtsoe of the Quorum of the Twelve Apostles said: "It is a paradox that men will gladly devote time every day for many years to learn a science or an art; yet will expect to win a knowledge of the gospel, which comprehends all sciences and arts, through perfunctory glances at books or occasional listening to sermons. The gospel should be studied more intensively than any school or college subject."[9]

LIVE THE PLAN We invite you to place your scripture study as the top priority in your studies. Before you do any of your school homework, we invite you to study your scriptures *first* to show God that gaining spiritual knowledge is your main priority. (The added benefit is that you'll no longer need to use the common excuse of not having enough time to study your scriptures.)

Develop Godlike Attributes

One of the reasons why Jesus came to earth is to show us what God the Father is like—how He would act and be (see John 14:7–9). Therefore, when we talk about trying to be like Jesus, we are also talking about trying to be like our Heavenly Father.

One way we can do that is by overcoming the tendencies of the "natural man" (Mosiah 3:19). President David O. McKay said, "One chief purpose of life is to overcome evil tendencies, to govern our appetites, to control our passions—anger, hatred, jealousy, immorality. We have to overcome them; we have to subject them, conquer them."[10]

Perhaps the most important positive attribute we can develop is love. After all, "God is love" (1 John 4:8). In fact, the two great commandments pertain to love. When the Savior was asked what the greatest commandments were, He said, "Thou shalt love the Lord thy God with all thy heart, and with all thy soul, and with all thy mind. This is the first and great commandment. And the second is like unto it, Thou shalt love thy neighbour as thyself" (Matthew 22:37–39). One of our great opportunities in life is to develop God's attribute of love.

Service is a fundamental way we can develop this attribute. When we serve others we're serving God (see Mosiah 2:17), and whatever we do to others, we do to the Savior (see Matthew 25:40). When we provide service to others, is it because we *have* to or because we *want* to? Either way, doing service is good, but doing it because we want to, because we love those we are serving, is best. President Marion G. Romney said, "Service is not something we endure on this earth so we can earn the right to live in the celestial kingdom. Service is the very fiber of which an exalted life in the celestial kingdom is made."[11]

Establish an Eternal Marriage and Family

The family proclamation states clearly that "the family is ordained of God. Marriage between man and woman is essential to His eternal plan."[12] It makes logical sense that if we are here to become more like our Eternal Parents, then we too must become fathers and mothers, sealed to our spouse for eternity. That is why the scriptures teach that having an eternal marriage and being sealed to a spouse in the temple is necessary for exaltation and to become like God (see Doctrine and Covenants 131:1–4; 132:18–21).

As a matter of fact, the sealing ordinances available in the temple are so necessary to fulfilling the purpose of life that the scriptures teach that "the whole earth would be utterly wasted" without them (Doctrine and Covenants 2:3). General Relief Society President Julie B. Beck taught, "When we speak of qualifying for the blessings of eternal life, we mean qualifying for the blessings of eternal families. . . . Without these blessings, the earth is wasted. . . . Without the family, there is no plan; there is no reason for it."[13]

Come unto Christ and Be Perfected in Him

The commandment to be perfect like God (see Matthew 5:48) is impossible to fulfill by ourselves. But through the atonement of Jesus Christ, we can be made perfect and holy. The prophet Moroni ended the Book of Mormon with this plea: "Yea, come unto Christ, and be perfected *in him*" (Moroni 10:32; emphasis added). That means that we must have faith in Him, repent of our sins, and make and keep covenants with Him until the end of our lives. It is through these sacred covenants that we become joined with Christ and can be perfected through Him (see chapter 9), enabling us to become like God.

Elder Richard G. Scott summarized almost all the points discussed in this chapter by saying,

The primary purpose of life . . . is to prove yourself obedient to the commandments of the Lord and thereby grow in understanding, capacity, and every worthy trait. It is to receive every required ordinance and to make and keep every needed covenant. It is to form and nourish a family. This experience includes having periods of trial and happiness, with the objective of returning triumphantly, having met well the challenges and opportunities of mortal life to receive the glorious blessings promised for such obedience.[14]

President Howard W. Hunter also promised, "As we attend the temple, we learn more richly and deeply the purpose of life."[15]

We testify that this life does have a divine purpose and a divine plan. It is the great "plan of our God" (2 Nephi 9:13) that enables us to become like Him.

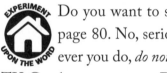 Do you want to see something really cool? Turn to page 80. No, seriously, turn there. Okay, now, whatever you do, *do not* read the next paragraph. Go watch TV. Go clean your room. Do something else.

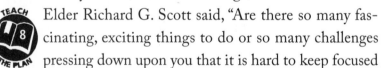 Elder Richard G. Scott said, "Are there so many fascinating, exciting things to do or so many challenges pressing down upon you that it is hard to keep focused on that which is essential? When things of the world crowd in, all too often the wrong things take highest priority. Then it is easy to forget the fundamental purpose of life. Satan has a powerful tool to use against good people. It is distraction. He would have good people fill life with 'good things' so there is no room for the essential ones. Have you unconsciously been caught in that trap?"[16]

Were we able to distract you from reading that paragraph? Don't be distracted from the true purposes of life!

Still Have Questions?

Why are we tempted if God wants us to be
righteous and become like Him?

Do you remember when they used to have "shopping sprees" on television? Someone would win a shopping spree and they would have five minutes to run through a store and grab anything they wanted, and they got to keep everything they put in their shopping cart. Sometimes it was frustrating to see what people grabbed. They would blow right past the sporting goods section and grab bed-spreads and pillows. Or they would ignore the candy aisle and stack up the cart with toothbrushes! What were they thinking?

Actually, the beauty of the shopping spree is this: Whatever is in the cart at the final checkout truly reflects a person's desires and priorities. With all the options available to them, if a person ignores the hiking boots and picks up some flip-flops, it's because she really wanted flip-flops. If the whole store contained only hiking boots, the person might choose hiking boots not because she loves to hike, but simply because what she really wanted wasn't available.

Life is a little like a spiritual shopping spree. God allows both good and evil, righteousness and sin, on the earth, and whatever we put in the cart of our lives is what we truly desire. If alcohol and pornography and sin are on the aisles, but we pass them up and instead fill our lives with moral purity, then it shows God what we truly desire. When we pass up the immodest clothing rack and in-stead fill our spiritual shopping cart (or literal one!) with modesty, it shows what we truly desire.

When we show up at the checkout line at the final judgment and God looks in the cart of our life, whatever we have filled it with will reflect our true priorities and character. If God did not allow temptation, we wouldn't have choice. "For it must needs be, that there is an opposition in all things. If not so . . . righteousness could not be brought to pass, neither wickedness, neither holiness nor misery, neither good nor bad" (2 Nephi 2:11).

What is the hardest test or trial to go through?

According to President Boyd K. Packer, for some people, the hardest spiritual tests aren't tragedies, but "ease and luxury."[17] Elder A. Theodore Tuttle of the First Council of the Seventy agreed and said that "the trials through which today's young people are passing—ease and luxury—may be the most severe test of any age."[18] During our times of supposed "prosperity," let us not be like so many of those in the past (and present) who forget God, succumb to pride, and fall into sin. By always remembering God and being humble, we can pass the hardest spiritual test of all—ease and luxury!

Teach the Plan!

What Is the Purpose of Our Life?

Objective: To help learners understand that their life has a divine, Godlike purpose, and how to fulfill that purpose.

Attention Getter: Teach the Plan #1: Ask your children the question, "What is the purpose of life?" Let each child share an answer to this foundational question. Then share the answer to this question as outlined in Teach the Plan #2.

Lesson Activity: Teach the Plan #3: Have your family explain the five truths about God that help us understand what it means to become like God. Go to http://seek.deseretbook.com/bigpicture and download a handout that has each of the five truths on its own page. Give one page to five different people in your family. Let each read the page and then summarize what they read for the other family members. Then ask the following discussion questions.

Discussion Questions: The following questions may help your children in understanding, identifying, and applying some gospel truths related to the purpose of life:

Teach the Plan #4: "How does understanding the fact that God has a glorified, perfected body affect how you want to treat your body?"

Teach the Plan #5: "What do you think you could do to increase your efforts to seek light and truth?"

Teach the Plan #6: "What are some connections you see between doing service and increasing in love?"

Teach the Plan #7: "How do you think establishing an eternal family relates to the purpose of life?"

Teach the Plan #9: "How might trials help us to fulfill our purpose in life?"

Activity: Do the Experiment upon the Word activity. Feel free to modify it and use another object lesson that demonstrates how distraction works. For example, ask half the family to sing one hymn, while the other half of the family sings a different hymn. Then read Elder Richard G. Scott's quote next to Teach the Plan #8. Ask your children, "How does Satan try to distract us from the purpose of life?"

Invitation to Act: Invite your children to do the Live the Plan activity and put their scripture study as a priority. Encourage them to keep a list of blessings they receive as a result.

7

Agency: Our Power to Act!

TEACH THE PLAN 1 "It's my life—I can do whatever I want!"

"My mom makes me so mad!"

"If I have my agency, then why do my parents tell me what to do?"

"I can't go to Mutual; I have to finish my homework."

Have you ever heard or said any of those statements? Each of them reflects a misunderstanding of what agency is and why we have been given it. What is agency? President David O. McKay frequently referred to agency as "God's greatest gift to man."[1] Simply stated, agency is "the ability and privilege God gives people to choose and to act for themselves."[2]

TEACH THE PLAN 2 In *Gospel Principles*, we read, "When we follow the temptations of Satan, we limit our choices. The following example suggests how this works. Imagine seeing a sign on the seashore that reads: 'Danger—whirlpool. No swimming allowed here.' We might think that is a restriction. But is it? We still have many choices. We are free to swim somewhere else. We are free to walk along the beach and pick up seashells. We are free to watch the sunset. We are free to go home. We are also free to ignore the sign and swim in the dangerous place. But once the whirlpool has us in its grasp and we are pulled under, we have very few choices. We can try to escape, or we can call for help, but we may drown."[3]

In order for agency to take effect certain conditions have to be present. We'll call these the four pillars of agency: Law, Knowledge of Good and Evil, Opposition, and the Power to Choose. Let's check them out with the help of the prophet Lehi's great discourse that he gave to his sons in 2 Nephi 2.

The Four Pillars of Agency

 Let's use an analogy to see how these four pillars are necessary for agency to exist.

Law

Suppose we offered you a can of beer and a can of lemonade.

Now imagine that the Word of Wisdom had never been given, and there was no prophetic or legal guidance on drinking alcohol. You wouldn't be able to choose which of the two drinks was the "right" drink because there would be no eternal law. The prophet Lehi taught that if "there is no law . . . there is no sin" (2 Nephi 2:13). But, as Lehi's son Jacob taught, God "has given a law" (2 Nephi 9:25). Having designated laws of God is a key part of our ability to exercise our agency. The law designates which choice is right.

Knowledge of Good and Evil

Have you ever done something wrong and didn't know it was wrong? This happens all the time in our youth, and especially with little children. (Bless their little souls, they have no idea it's wrong to color the walls with lipstick.) It isn't until we know something is right or wrong that we can purposefully choose to obey or disobey the law and therefore be accountable for our righteousness or wickedness.

Using these same two drinks, we can illustrate the importance of knowledge of good and evil in terms of exercising agency. Even if God has designated the law (don't drink alcohol), if we don't know what God's law is, we will be less able to make the right choice. The scriptures teach us that because of the light of Christ, "men are instructed sufficiently that they know good from evil" (2 Nephi 2:5).

Opposition

Now suppose we offered you two drinks to choose between, but both were cans of beer. Well, another key part of agency is having choices that are in opposition to each other. If our only choice is between two cans of the same beer, then it's pretty hard to exercise our agency. The prophet Lehi taught us: "For it must needs be, that there is an opposition in all things. If not so . . . righteousness could not be brought to pass, neither wickedness" (2 Nephi 2:11). Having choices that are in opposition to each other gives us the opportunity to exercise our agency and make the right choice.

Power to Choose

Let's consider one last pillar of agency: the power to choose. Even if we have a law, a knowledge of the law, and opposites to choose between, if we are not able to choose we cannot exercise our agency. Even if we know the lemonade is the correct choice, if the lemonade is put impossibly out of our reach and we are forced to drink the beer, we cannot exercise our agency because we have no power to do so. Without the power to choose what we will do, there can be no agency and therefore no accountability. Thankfully, God has given us the power to choose, teaching us that we "are free to choose" (2 Nephi 2:27).

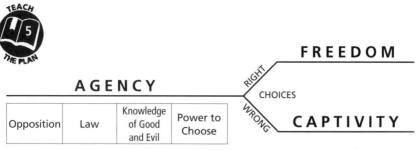

What Does Agency Have to Do with Me?

There are lots of ways that the doctrine of agency affects us in our lives. Elder Robert D. Hales taught, "Some may remember the old adage: 'The devil made me do it.' Today I want to convey, in absolutely certain terms, that the adversary cannot make us do anything."[4]

Perhaps the greatest blessing of agency is that we are free to make our own choices and control our own destiny. The prophets teach us, "Heavenly Father has given you agency, the ability to choose right from wrong and to act for yourself. Next to the bestowal of life itself, the right to direct your life is one of God's greatest gifts to you."[5] However, with that freedom comes responsibility. The prophets call this "accountability" and teach that "you are responsible for the choices you make."[6]

Let's look at how we can be better, more responsible agents.

Agency and Excuses

When we truly understand agency, we realize that when we make excuses we are denying our agency. We are saying that something or someone else controls us and our actions and that we aren't in control, which is contrary to the doctrine of agency. When we make an excuse, we are saying that we don't have a choice in the thing we are making an excuse for and thus we deny our power to choose.

For example, at a youth dance a young man asks a young woman to dance and she says, "I'd love to dance with you, but I can't. I have to go talk to my friend about something." She is essentially saying, "I don't have a choice, I *have* to talk to my friend. I'd love to dance with you if I could, but I *can't*." By making an excuse, she denies her power to choose and her control over her behavior, which she is responsible for independent of any other person.

Here's another example: A young man is asked by his seminary teacher if he read his scriptures. He says, "I couldn't because I had so much homework and was too tired at the end of the night." We hope his seminary teacher would correct the incorrect agency statement with something like "You mean, you *chose* not to study your scriptures because you *chose* to do your homework, eat dinner, and play basketball before studying your scriptures?"

When you get right down to it, most excuses are an attack on one of the four pillars of agency. Consider this quote from Elder Paul V. Johnson: "Think of some of the excuses people give for their wrong actions: 'I didn't know it was wrong'— a claim they had no knowledge of good from evil. 'I couldn't help it'—claiming they had no personal power to choose. 'There wasn't anything else I could do'—purporting no choices from which to pick. 'Don't push your morals on me'—assuming there is no eternal law."[7]

Here is a key principle: when we make excuses, we weaken ourselves. Making excuses hurts us because by attacking those pillars of agency we trick ourselves into thinking that we really *aren't* free to choose, or that there is no real eternal law. We should avoid making excuses. Alma taught his son, "Do not endeavor to excuse yourself *in the least point*" (Alma 42:30; emphasis added). The moment we take responsibility for our actions is the moment we gain power over the course of our lives.

No Excuses

Look at the following statements and figure out which ones deny agency:

- My little sister is such a pest. She really makes me mad.
- I'd love to go on a date with you, but the truth is that I have to stay home with my sick cat and comfort her.
- I won't sub for you, because I will not work on Sundays.
- Sorry, that's just the way I am.

- I'm sorry, I can't go out with you, I have to wash my hair.
- I was going to read the Book of Mormon but I couldn't. The dog ate my scriptures.
- That offends me.
- I choose not to watch R-rated movies.
- I want to do missionary work but I can't. I'm too shy.
- I can't stop thinking about it.
- I'm sorry this is late. It's my fault; I'll do better next time.

 Scan this QR Code or visit http://www.youtube.com/watch?v=gWQ5dPeixdw to see the powerful effects of what our agency can lead to.

Take the "No Excuses Challenge" for twenty-four hours. Refrain from phrases like "I have to" or "He made me" or "I couldn't help it." What changes do you notice in your life because you took this challenge?

Agency and Emotions

One area of agency that is sometimes overlooked is that to a large extent we *choose* our emotions. Try the following experiment to see what we mean.

Alright, get ready to loosen up your facial muscles and give the biggest, cheesiest smile ever. (This activity works best if you have other people do it with you.) Now, give your best smile for a full minute. Ready, set, go!

> If you smiled for a full minute, odds are you feel better. You may have even laughed with each other. Notice how something as simple as choosing to smile affected you? We can choose our attitudes, and we can choose to smile!

Here are a few of the emotions we can choose:

We have the power to choose the emotion of happiness. President Harold B. Lee taught, "Happiness does not depend on what happens outside of you but on what happens inside of you; it is measured by the spirit with which you meet the problems of life."[8]

 Now consider the emotion of anger. Can anybody *make* us mad? President Thomas S. Monson answered this question saying, "No one can *make* us angry. It is our choice. If we desire to have a proper spirit with us at all times, we must choose to refrain from becoming angry. I testify that such is possible."[9]

Sometimes people say that something "offends them." Can something offend us, or are we choosing to take offense? Elder David A. Bednar taught, "It ultimately is impossible for another person to offend you or to offend me. Indeed, believing that another person offended us is fundamentally false. To be offended is a *choice* we make; it is not a *condition* inflicted or imposed upon us by someone or something else."[10]

Another example of an emotion we can choose is "love." Sometimes we hear a married person say they "fell out of love" with their spouse. Is that true? Can we "fall out of love," or do we choose to stop loving somebody?

Elder Lynn G. Robbins answered this question by saying, "Any commandment by God involves agency. We can obey or disobey, but there is always a choice. When the Lord uses the command form of the verb love in 'Thou shalt love thy wife with all [thy] heart, and

Gotcha! Now turn back to page 70.

shall cleave unto her and none else' (Doctrine and Covenants 42:22), He is not leaving this love in Cupid's hands. . . . You can't fall out of love if it's a commandment to stay in love."[11]

How Would You Feel in a Nazi Concentration Camp?

 Are you in control of how you feel? Could you control your feelings even if you were in a Nazi concentration camp? A man named Viktor Frankl was in a concentration camp, and he wrote,

> We who lived in concentration camps can remember the men who walked through the huts comforting others, giving away their last piece of bread. They may have been few in number, but they offer sufficient proof that everything can be taken from a man but one thing: the last of the human freedoms—to choose one's attitude in any given set of circumstances, to choose one's own way.[12]

 Take the "No Anger Challenge" for twenty-four hours. Can you choose not to be angry for twenty-four straight hours? How long can you go?

Acting as Agents

A key part of understanding agency is that we are "agents." To be an agent means we are authorized to act. God has "given unto the children of men to be agents unto themselves" (Doctrine and Covenants 104:17), which means we should be responsible for the things God has given us.

We are agents over our choices, our bodies, our attitudes, our time, our talents, our resources, and much, much more. Being an agent means that we don't just avoid bad things, we proactively choose to do good (meaning nobody has to tell us to do it). The Lord has said,

For behold, it is not meet that I should command in all things; for he that is compelled in all things, the same is a slothful and not a wise servant; wherefore he receiveth no reward.

Verily I say, men should be anxiously engaged in a good cause, and do many things of their own free will, and bring to pass much righteousness;

For the power is in them, wherein they are agents unto themselves. And inasmuch as men do good they shall in nowise lose their reward. (Doctrine and Covenants 58:26–28)

Let us never forget that God has given us our agency. We have the ability to act and not merely to be acted upon (see 2 Nephi 2:14). Let us choose to be good agents by choosing to "use [our] agency to show [our] love for God by keeping His commandments."[13]

Still Have Questions?

Why does my agency matter if God already knows everything I will do?

God does know what is going to happen to us ahead of time (see Abraham 2:8), but that doesn't mean we "have" to do it. (See chapter 4.) For example, are you going to close this book right now, or are you going to keep reading? We're not sure what you're going to do, but God knows. Still, it's your choice whether you close the book or not.

Just because God knows does not mean He is choosing for you. Understanding how God knows what we will do without forcing us to do it is difficult to grasp. In fact, even Elder Richard G. Scott said that he didn't fully comprehend it. He said, "The Lord has placed currents of divine influence in your life that will lead you along the individual plan He would have you fulfill here on earth. . . . I do not fully understand how it is done, but this divine current does not take away your moral agency. You can make the decisions you choose to make."[14]

Teach the Plan!

Agency: Our Power to Act!

Objective: To help learners understand what agency is and how they can appropriately exercise agency in their lives.

Attention Getter: Share the excuses next to Teach the Plan #1 and then ask your children, "What is agency?"

Visual: Teach the Plan #2: Show your children a "No swimming" sign. Then ask your children whether this sign restricts their ability to choose or helps them with their ability to choose.

Object Lesson: Involve one or more children in the activities illustrating the four pillars of agency next to Teach the Plan #3. Have them choose which of the two drinks they want—the lemonade or the beer. (Wrap a piece of paper around a can of soda and label it "beer" for the demonstration.)

For younger children (ages five to ten years old), illustrate the principle next to Teach the Plan #4 by placing the can of lemonade in an impossible place for them to reach and then asking one of your kids to be righteous and get the can of lemonade and drink it.

Visual: Ask one of your children to explain the diagram next to Teach the Plan #5 in his or her own words.

Lesson Activity: Teach the Plan #6: Have your kids list ten common excuses (or excuses they have used recently). Then read Elder Paul V. Johnson's quote. Review the excuses that your children came up with and ask your children to identify which aspects of agency are being attacked by those excuses.

Discussion Question: Teach the Plan #7: "Why do you think that the moment we take responsibility for our actions is the moment we gain power over the direction of our lives?"

Lesson Activity: The activity next to Teach the Plan #8 can be a fun exercise to make sure your kids understand the connection between agency and making excuses.

Video: Watch the video linked at Teach the Plan #9, but be aware that the topic of the video (pornography) may not be appropriate for younger children.

Invitation to Act: Invite your children to accept the twenty-four-hour "No Excuses Challenge" at the Live the Plan icon. Take the challenge yourself as well. Follow up with your family in twenty-four hours and discuss what you learned.

Teach the Plan!

Agency and Emotions

Objective: To help learners understand the connection between agency and emotion.

Attention Getter: Do the Experiment upon the Word activity and then read the quote by President Harold B. Lee.

Lesson Activity: Teach the Plan #10 gives quotes from talks by President Thomas S. Monson, Elder David A. Bednar, and Elder Lynn G. Robbins that focus on different aspects of agency and emotions. Have each child read one of the quotes from this section and then give a summary to the rest of the family. If you want to have a more in-depth discussion on this topic, have your children read the entire talks before giving their summaries to the rest of the family.

Visual: Teach the Plan #11: Show an image from a concentration camp and ask your kids if they think they could still choose to have a positive attitude in such terrible circumstances. After they share their thoughts, discuss how they might be able to choose to have a good attitude in their life even when things aren't perfect. Then read the quote from Viktor Frankl.

Invitation to Act: Invite your children to accept the twenty-four-hour "No Anger Challenge" at the Live the Plan icon. Take the challenge yourself as well. Follow up with your family in twenty-four hours and discuss what you learned.

8

God's Greatest Gift: The Atonement of Jesus Christ

Have you ever wondered why the hymn "I Need Thee Every Hour"[1] says that we need Jesus every *hour*? Sometimes people think, "Well, I need Jesus when I sin and need to be forgiven, and I'll need Jesus when I'm resurrected. But I don't sin or need to be resurrected every *hour*. So why do I need him every hour of my life?" Hopefully, this chapter will help us all see that we don't need Jesus every hour, we need him every *second!*

Consider the following real-life situations:

Young woman #1: "I don't commit any serious sins, and I think I'm a good person. I know the Atonement applies to people who have sinned and need forgiveness, and because I'm pretty good it seems like I don't need it as much as others. I know that sounds bad. I know I'm not perfect, but it seems like I don't appreciate the Atonement like I should."

Young man #1: "My father left when I was five and even though I'm only fifteen I have to work to pay the bills. I get so tired after going to school, and then working until midnight every night. I see other kids at school and they don't have the problems I do. My mom tries to understand me but I don't want to burden her with all my problems—she has enough of her own. I feel so alone. What can I do?"

Young woman #2: "My life has been really hard. I was diagnosed with cancer last year and the treatments I've been getting are really painful. Sometimes I want to give up. What can I do to have the strength to keep going?"

Young man #2: "I have messed up my life. I've done everything bad that you can do. I feel like I have no hope, and no point in going on. It is too late for me."

Although each of these four teenagers struggle with different problems, the answer to their concerns lies in understanding the Atonement of Jesus Christ and applying what it can do for us in our everyday lives.

What Is the Atonement of Jesus Christ?

To *atone* means to make something right, or to reconcile it. The primary purpose and meaning of the Atonement is to make us right before God, or to "be reconciled unto [God] through the atonement of Christ" (Jacob 4:11). In essence we are separated from God by both death and sin. When Adam and Eve partook of the forbidden fruit, both physical death (mortality) and spiritual death (sin) entered the world. *True to the Faith* teaches that "as descendants of Adam and Eve, all people inherit the effects of the Fall. We all experience spiritual death, being separated from the presence of God, and we are all subject to temporal death, which is the death of the physical body."[2]

If we are to live with or become like God, we need to be both sinless and immortal like He is. The problem is that you and I cannot cleanse ourselves from sin, and we can't resurrect ourselves. We need someone else to do that for us. We need someone else to reconcile us. That is where the Atonement of Jesus Christ comes in. Only He could do it, because He was sinless and perfect.

Jesus was also the only one who could overcome death. Jesus inherited the mortal power to die from His mother Mary, and He inherited the power to resurrect and overcome death from His Heavenly Father. Jesus was uniquely qualified to help all of us overcome sin and death, and because He loves us and loves the Father, Jesus voluntarily suffered in the Garden of Gethsemane beyond what we can imagine as He paid the price to justice for our sins. The suffering was so great that Jesus said it caused Him "to tremble because of pain, and to bleed at every pore, and to suffer both body and spirit" (Doctrine and Covenants 19:18). Afterward, Jesus voluntarily submitted himself to the Roman soldiers and "was crucified, died, and rose again the third day" (Doctrine and Covenants 20:23), thus shattering the bands of death for all of God's children and providing the power of resurrection.

We love Jesus for doing this! Without Him and His loving Atonement, "all mankind were in a lost and in a fallen state, and ever would be" (1 Nephi 10:6). But because of Him, we can overcome sin and death, and fulfill our potential as children of God to become like God and live with Him again. Without Jesus, the purpose of the plan of salvation fails (see Moses 1:39).

What Would Have Happened to Us If There Had Been No Atonement?

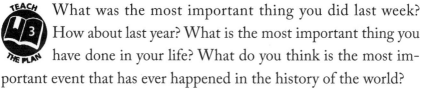 What was the most important thing you did last week? How about last year? What is the most important thing you have done in your life? What do you think is the most important event that has ever happened in the history of the world?

Alma says that there is one event "of more importance than . . . all" (Alma 7:7) and that is the Atonement of Jesus Christ (see Alma 7:7–13). Why? Because without the Atonement, the whole plan of salvation wouldn't work. We would have forever remained dead and in our sins, and "our spirits must become subject to . . . the devil, to rise no more. And our spirits must have become like unto him, and we become devils, angels to a devil, to be shut out from the presence of our God, and to remain with the father of lies, in misery, like unto himself" (2 Nephi 9:8–9).

Thankfully, the greatest event in the history of the world happened—the Atonement of Christ—and we can be blessed by it every day.

What Does the Atonement Mean for Me?

No matter who we are, the Atonement applies to us on a daily basis. President Boyd K. Packer taught, "For some reason, we think the Atonement of Christ applies *only* at the end of mortal life. . . . It is much more than that. It is an ever-present power to call upon in everyday life. When we are . . . burdened with grief, He can heal us. . . . *The Atonement has practical, personal everyday value.*"[3]

 Let's look at how four aspects of the Atonement can help each of us daily:

1. The cleansing power of the Atonement.
2. The understanding power of the Atonement.
3. The strengthening power of the Atonement.
4. The converting power of the Atonement.

The Cleansing Power of the Atonement

Perhaps when we think of the Atonement we most often think of the power of Jesus Christ to cleanse us from sin. This is indeed a vital aspect of the Savior's sacrifice.

Alma testified, "The Son of God suffereth according to the flesh that he might take upon him the sins of his people, that he might blot out their transgressions according to the power of his deliverance" (Alma 7:13). Amulek further witnessed, "I do know that Christ shall come among the children of men, to take upon him the transgressions of his people, and that he shall atone for the sins of the world; for the Lord God hath spoken it" (Alma 34:8).

The first young woman described at the beginning of this chapter might not realize it, but she needs the Atonement just as much as a drug addict does. Let's use an analogy with clothing to help us see this. If we liken sin to dirt, we could imagine that the drug dealer's clothes are covered in mud. The young woman who is doing her best to keep the commandments might have only a few stains on her shirt. But neither one will be able to go to heaven, for as the Savior has said, "I the Lord cannot look upon sin with the least degree of allowance" (Doctrine and Covenants 1:31).

People who believe they don't need the cleansing power of the Atonement need to realize that "all have sinned, and come short of the glory of God" (Romans 3:23). This is not meant to drag us down or make anyone feel hopeless; rather, it is to remind us that we need to be humble and realize that even the "best" people need the cleansing power of the Atonement in their lives.

Similarly, there are some people (like the second young man from the beginning of the chapter) who think that they have sinned so much that it is impossible for them to ever be cleansed and made pure. They think that their sins are too serious, their mistakes too severe, their stains too dark and deep. We testify that the power of the Atonement is infinite (see 2 Nephi 9:7)—it can clean infinitely small sins, and infinitely large ones. If we haven't committed the unforgivable sin—which the average member cannot—then there is no sin the Atonement cannot cover. There is no hole Jesus cannot mend. There is no stain He cannot cleanse. "Though your sins be as scarlet, they shall be as white as snow; though they be red like crimson, they shall be as wool" (Isaiah 1:18).

Remember, even great prophets like Alma the Younger and the sons of Mosiah were once "the very vilest of sinners" (Mosiah 28:4), and the Lord forgave, changed, and redeemed them. If we come unto Christ in faith each day, and repent, He can redeem us too, no matter how serious the sin.

Whether we have big sins to battle, or little sins to overcome, we all need to repent daily. President Henry B. Eyring said, "One of the questions we must ask of our Heavenly Father in private prayer is this:

'What have I done today, or not done, which displeases Thee? If I can only know, I will repent with all my heart without delay.' That humble prayer will be answered."[4] As we follow President Eyring's advice, we will understand what we should stop or start doing. As we follow these impressions, repent, and make daily changes for the better, we will feel the cleansing power of the Atonement in our lives.

 Elder D. Todd Christofferson shared the following story, which shows how even things we think are small, are still important.

In my youth I once was negligent in a way that later caused an injury to one of my brothers. It was not major, but required some stitches in his hand. I was embarrassed about it, and did not own up to my stupidity at the time, and no one ever knew about my role in the matter. Many years later, I was praying that God would reveal to me anything in my life that needed correction so that I might be found more acceptable before Him, and this incident came to my mind. Frankly, I had forgotten all about it. The Spirit whispered to me that this was an unresolved transgression that I needed to confess. I called my brother and apologized and asked for his forgiveness which he promptly and generously gave. . . .

It was interesting and very significant to me that the Lord had not forgotten about that event of the distant past even though I had. It was a comparatively small thing, but it still needed to be handled, or I would be answering for it at the judgment bar when the opportunity for repentance had passed. I realized once again that things do not get "swept under the rug" in the eternal economy of things. Sins do not take care of themselves or simply fade away. They must be dealt with, and the wonderful thing is that because of His atoning grace they can be dealt with in a much happier and less painful manner than directly satisfying offended justice ourselves.[5]

The Understanding Power of the Atonement

Another way we can feel the power of the Atonement in our lives comes when we realize that Jesus understands everything about our lives because He has experienced it. He knows what we are going through because *He went through it.* Alma said that the Savior would "go forth, suffering pains and afflictions and temptations *of every kind*; and this that the word might be fulfilled which saith he will take upon him the pains and the sicknesses of his people" (Alma 7:11; emphasis added). Similarly Isaiah wrote that Christ "hath borne our griefs, and carried our sorrows" (Isaiah 53:4). If we feel like nobody can understand our situation, we are wrong. Christ does. And as we turn to Him in times of trial, we can feel of His love and understanding and apply this aspect of the Atonement in our lives.

 Consider how Anne was able to feel the effects of the Atonement in her life and how it helped her overcome a difficult trial she faced.

I was eight years old when my parents divorced. I remember the day my dad moved out. It seemed like everything I knew about life fell to pieces after that. I was confused, lonely, and sad. It felt like a big part of me had been ripped out. . . .

As I got older, the hole inside me became a deep pit of sadness. I tried to fill it with all sorts of things: relationships, school, rebellion, even too much food. None of those things worked. . . .

. . . I had nowhere left to turn except to Christ. Night after night I knelt in prayer and asked my Heavenly Father, in the name of Jesus Christ, to heal my emptiness. . . .

. . . Little by little Heavenly Father intervened in my life to show me that Christ's love *was* healing me. Heavenly Father also let me know He loves me, He knows me, and He wants me to have an eternal family.

I know, unmistakably now, that my Savior was aware of my pain and sadness. He never gave up on me. I can see now that He

strengthened me and carried me through those difficult times. . . .
It was Christ who healed my heart.[6]

Whatever problems, whatever hardships, whatever frustrations, or whatever sadness we have had, the Savior has experienced it as well. Why did the Savior do all this? Alma taught that Christ did this so "that his bowels may be filled with mercy, according to the flesh, that he may know according to the flesh how to succor his people according to their infirmities" (Alma 7:12). Bishop Merrill J. Bateman said, "In the garden and on the cross, Jesus saw each of us and not only bore our sins, but also experienced our deepest feelings so that he would know how to comfort and strengthen us."[7]

The Strengthening Power of the Atonement

Some people may not realize that there is power in the Atonement not only to help us overcome sin but also to strengthen us to do good, righteous things that we could not otherwise accomplish with our own capabilities. Elder David A. Bednar said, "Most of us clearly understand that the Atonement is for sinners. I am not so sure, however, that we know and understand that the Atonement is also for saints—for good men and women who are obedient and worthy and conscientious and who are striving to become better and serve more faithfully."[8]

The Bible Dictionary uses the word "grace" to explain that through the Atonement of Christ we can be given "divine means of help or strength . . . an enabling power."[9] The enabling power of the Atonement gives us ability beyond our natural capacity to do things we otherwise couldn't accomplish on our own. It was the enabling power of the Atonement that gave Nephi the ability to build the boat, that allowed Peter to walk on water, that gave Joseph Smith the ability to translate the Book of Mormon. That same strengthening power from the Atonement can be given to us in our daily lives to make us better in all that we do.

Suppose for example that you are trying to overcome a bad temper. You can use lots of great techniques like breathing deeply or counting to ten. And you can also pray and ask for the power of the Atonement to give you strength to control your emotions and to change your nature to be more patient. When you have a church calling to perform, or even a homework assignment to do, you can pray for the strength of the Lord to help you accomplish it.

In Alma 31, Alma and his fellow missionaries faced a difficult challenge, but they knew the Savior could strengthen them. Alma prayed, saying, "O Lord, wilt thou grant unto me that I may have strength" (Alma 31:31). Alma didn't pray for his trials to go away, he prayed for *strength*. The result of this prayer was that "the Lord . . . gave them strength" (Alma 31:38). The Lord not only gives prophets strength, but *True to the Faith* teaches us to "remember the strength you can receive through the enabling power of grace."[10] The Atonement can give *us* strength in our daily lives as well.

The Converting Power of the Atonement

The Atonement of Jesus Christ has the power to change our character. President Gordon B. Hinckley said the gospel—which is centered on the Atonement of Jesus Christ—"can change our very natures."[11] Jesus' Atonement can make bad people good, good people great, and great people into true saints. One of the purposes of this life is to gain Christlike attributes and become more like God, and a person can change "the natural man and [become] a saint through the atonement of Christ the Lord" (Mosiah 3:19). Each day as we seek for Christ's atoning assistance, He can transform us, change us, and make us holy, until "we have no more disposition to do evil, but to do good continually" (Mosiah 5:2). (See chapter 10.)

We testify that the Atonement of Jesus Christ is not only for serious sinners. It is not only for those who have died. It is not just for the young, or the old. It is not something that is only needed occasionally, or even every hour. As we come to more fully understand and rely on the Atonement of Jesus Christ, we begin to realize how it blesses our life in every aspect, and how we need Jesus every minute of every day.

EXPERIMENT Grab a handful of rocks from the yard (at least twenty) and place them in a bag. With your eyes UPON THE WORD closed, put your hand into the bag and pick one of the rocks. Now, *without looking* at the rock you have chosen, pull it out of the bag and *feel* it. Take a minute and just feel the rock—get to know its shape, texture, and nooks and crannies. Now, with your eyes still closed, put it back with the other rocks and shake the bag. Then, dump out the rocks and find your rock.

Did you find it? Odds are you did. How? What was probably the first thing you did? You picked up the rock and *felt it* so you could be sure that was the one. How does this relate to the Atonement? Although there are billions of different people, Christ knows each of us individually because He has *felt* the nooks, crannies, and shape of our lives (see Isaiah 53:4). He therefore knows us and can help us individually.

LIVE THE Because the Atonement is vital for everyone, we have a special challenge for you. Review this chapter and PLAN prepare a short lesson based on the question "What is the Atonement, and what does it mean to me?" Then, teach the lesson to somebody you know. You will strengthen the person you teach, and as you teach others about the Atonement, this doctrine will sink even deeper into your heart.

Still Have Questions?

Does God really care about me?

There are three scriptures that we love that answer this question. Please know that these words are the voice of the Lord directly to you. God has said, "I know thee by name" (Exodus 33:12), "I have loved thee with an everlasting love" (Jeremiah 31:3), and "I will never leave thee, nor forsake thee" (Hebrews 13:5). We testify to you that God knows your name, He loves you, and He will never leave you. *He loves you.* He has promised, "I will not leave you comfortless: I will come to you" (John 14:18). We know this promise is true.

I've been praying for strength, but my life is still hard. What can I do to have the strength to keep going?

 The prophet Nephi also faced a series of difficult struggles. Once his brothers tied him up with cords and left him in the wilderness to be eaten by wild beasts. Nephi wrote,

> But it came to pass that I prayed unto the Lord, saying: O Lord, according to my faith which is in thee, wilt thou deliver me from the hands of my brethren; yea, even give me strength that I may burst these bands with which I am bound.
>
> And it came to pass that when I had said these words, behold, the bands were loosed from off my hands and feet. (1 Nephi 7:17–18)

When we were younger, we used to think that Nephi became like a superhero and broke the ropes with one mighty pull. But Elder David A. Bednar taught,

> I personally do not believe the bands with which Nephi was bound just magically fell from his hands and wrists. Rather, I suspect he was blessed with both persistence and personal strength beyond his natural capacity, that he then "in the strength of the

Lord" (Mosiah 9:17) worked and twisted and tugged on the cords and ultimately and literally was enabled to break the bands. . . .

. . . As you and I come to understand and employ the enabling power of the Atonement in our personal lives, we will pray and seek for strength to change our circumstances rather than praying for our circumstances to be changed.[12]

The Lord gave Nephi the strength to keep twisting and tugging on those ropes. He will give you the strength to move forward in your difficult circumstances. Remember the Atonement is not only to cleanse us from sin, it is also to strengthen us and give us the power to do things we could not accomplish with our own capabilities.

What if I've done too many bad things to ever be forgiven?

First, we need to understand that Christ's Atonement is infinite. (That's more than a duotrigintillion googolplex—which is a real number, by the way!)

Something that is "infinite" has no beginning and no end. You cannot take anything away from it, and you can't add anything to it. It is *infinite*.

The scriptures teach us that Jesus Christ's Atonement is "an infinite atonement" (2 Nephi 9:7; Alma 34:12). In other words, Christ's power to help you in your life has no end. It goes on forever. Whatever sins you have committed, whatever trials you have had, whatever strength you need, Christ has the power to heal, lift, cleanse, and empower you. He will not run out of strength. His power is truly infinite; you can always count on Him.

My Christian friends ask if Mormons believe in "being saved by grace." Do we?

Being saved by grace simply means "the divine help and strength we receive through the Atonement of the Lord Jesus Christ."[13] That help includes the ability to do good works, receive forgiveness for our sins, and be blessed by the power of resurrection—all of which comes through the grace of Christ and makes it possible for us to go to heaven.

In fact, being saved by grace is one of the central themes of the Book of Mormon. Lehi taught, "There is no flesh that can dwell in the presence of God, save it be through the merits, and mercy, and grace of the Holy Messiah" (2 Nephi 2:8). Jacob taught, "It is only in and through the grace of God that ye are saved" (2 Nephi 10:24). Nephi said, "For we know that it is by grace that we are saved, after all we can do" (2 Nephi 25:23). And Moroni closed the Book of Mormon by saying, "By the grace of God ye are perfect in Christ" (Moroni 10:32).

Although your friends might understand the doctrine of grace differently than you do, you can truthfully say, "Mormons believe in Christ's grace, and I believe that it is only through the grace of Christ that I can go to heaven."

 Scan this QR code or visit http://www .youtube.com/watch?v=EpFhS0dAduc to hear one apostle's testimony of the power of Christ's Atonement.

Scan this QR code or visit https://lds.org/youth /video/he-will-give-you-help to see how the Atonement helped one young man through a difficult trial.

Teach the Plan!

God's Greatest Gift: The Atonement of Jesus Christ

Objective: To help learners understand both what the doctrine of the Atonement is and how it can change their lives.

Attention Getter: Teach the Plan #1: Read the scenarios given by the four teenagers. Ask your family how they think the Atonement could help each of these individuals. After you have studied about the various powers of the Atonement, ask your children which aspects of the Atonement might apply to each situation.

Discussion Question: Ask your children to respond to the question, "What is the Atonement of Jesus Christ?" The discussion following Teach the Plan #2 contains possible answers to this question.

Visual: Teach the Plan #3: Ask your children to draw a picture of what they think might be the most important event in history. After reviewing the pictures, ask, "Why is the Atonement the greatest event that has ever happened in the history of the world?"

Lesson Activity: Teach the Plan #4: Have your family explain the four aspects of the Savior's Atonement. Go to http://seek.deseretbook.com/bigpicture and download a handout that has each section on its own page. Give one page to four different people in your family. Let each read their page and then have them teach the other family members what they learned. Remember to include and answer the following discussion questions.

Discussion Questions: The following questions may help your children in understanding, identifying, and applying some gospel truths related to the Atonement of Jesus Christ:

Teach the Plan #5: "How does the story from Elder D. Todd Christofferson help us understand that we need to repent of even small sins?"

Teach the Plan #6: "How did Anne experience the understanding power of the Atonement? How have you experienced this power in your life?"

Teach the Plan #7: "How has the Atonement of Jesus Christ given you strength?"

Teach the Plan #8: "How can the Savior's Atonement change our very natures? How has the Atonement changed parts of your nature?"

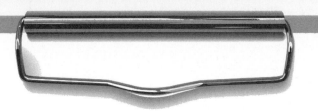

Object Lesson: Do the Experiment upon the Word activity. Afterward, share your testimony with your family about how Christ knows and loves each of us individually. Invite others to bear their testimony as well.

Role-Play: Teach the Plan #9: Have your children role-play Nephi's experience of breaking the bands. Were your children successful with one big burst? Or were constant, persistent tugs more useful? Read the quote by Elder David A. Bednar, and then ask, "How does this relate to the strengthening power of the Atonement?"

Videos: Watch one or both of the video clips at Teach the Plan #10.

Invitation to Act: Encourage your children to accept the invitation offered at the Live the Plan icon. Consider if there is a person or family that you could invite into your home to be taught by your children. Such an individual could be an investigator, a less-active member, or a widow in the ward who would be willing to be taught by your children.

9

Connected to Christ by Covenants

 Pop quiz time! Get your pencils and a piece of paper out and get ready to write. In sixty seconds we want you to list everything—and we mean *everything*—that needs to be done in order to be saved in the celestial kingdom. Ready, set, go!

So, how long was your list of celestial requirements? Did it look something like this?

- Pay my tithing
- Fast (oh, and pay a generous fast offering!)
- Go to church each week
- Study my scriptures
- Say my prayers (three times daily)
- Be nice to other people
- Don't cheat in school
- Serve well in my calling
- Go home teaching
- Don't smoke
- Go to bed early—wake up early
- Go to seminary
- Watch general conference

 What would the list look like if Jesus were writing it? What would He say is required for us to be saved? Well, He did write one—in the scriptures. Here is His list in its entirety:

"He that believeth and is baptized shall be saved" (Mark 16:16). Wow. That list was huge. That probably took, like, five seconds to read. And just in case you think Jesus only said that once, think again. This same simple message—believe and be baptized to be saved—is repeated at least *thirteen* different times in the scriptures (see 2 Nephi 9:23; 3 Nephi 11:33–34; 3 Nephi 23:5; Mormon 9:23; Ether 4:18; Moroni 7:34; Doctrine and Covenants 68:9; 112:29). He must really want us to get that point!

Although there are many things we should do and need to do in order to become like God (see chapter 6), perhaps the most essential thing we need to do on this earth to fulfill the plan of salvation is simply this: make and keep covenants with Jesus Christ. As a matter of fact, the entire plan of salvation can be summarized like this: "We believe that through the Atonement of Christ, all mankind may be saved, by obedience to the laws and ordinances of the Gospel" (Articles of Faith 1:3).

Here is a little bit more about how that works, and why covenants and ordinances are essential for us to qualify for the celestial kingdom and to fulfill the plan of salvation.

Covenants and Ordinances

"A covenant is a sacred agreement between God and a person."[1] In other words, when we make a covenant we agree to the conditions God sets for us, and God promises us something in return. Covenants are everywhere in the scriptures. As a matter of fact, the Old Testament was originally called the Old Covenant, and the New Testament, the New Covenant.[2] One of the main purposes of the Book of Mormon is not only to testify of Jesus but also so that we "may know the covenants of the Lord" (title page of the Book of Mormon).

So what is God's covenant that He offers us? It is basically this:

You Agree to

- Take upon you the name of Christ
- Always remember Jesus
- Be willing to keep His commandments (see Doctrine and Covenants 20:37, 77)

God Agrees to

- Make you holy and clean and perfect through Jesus so that you can inherit the celestial kingdom of heaven and become like Him (see Moroni 10:33)

This covenant with God is not made by signing a contract or shaking hands, but by an *ordinance*—specifically, the ordinance of baptism.

In the Church, we make many covenants, each of which is connected to an ordinance. We make our first covenant with God at baptism (and we renew that covenant each week through the sacrament); worthy males make covenants when they receive the priesthood; and faithful adult members make the most sacred and holy covenants in the Church when they enter the temple to receive their endowment and are sealed to their spouse. These various covenants are called "saving" covenants because they are necessary for a person to be saved and exalted in the celestial kingdom.

How Covenants Save Us

You might be wondering, "How does making and keeping a covenant with Jesus save me?" Perhaps a math analogy will help.

What does this symbol mean?

$$\infty$$

That's right: infinity. Something that is infinite means you cannot add to it, or take away from it. It has limitless capacity. If you add a number to infinity, no matter the size of the number, the answer is infinity.

$$50 + \infty = \infty$$

$$50,000 + \infty = \infty$$

So what does infinity have to do with covenants and being saved? The Book of Mormon describes Jesus' Atonement as "an infinite atonement" (2 Nephi 9:7; Alma 34:12), which means that there is no limit to Jesus' ability to save. Anything added to Jesus' Atonement becomes infinite as well. If our lives are joined with Jesus, then He will save us. If we are connected to Christ, then His perfection is connected to us.

The real question in the spiritual equation is this: What joins our lives with Jesus? How are we connected to His infinite Atonement? The answer is, of course, through covenants. Consider the math equation again:

Jesus' infinite Atonement (∞), plus covenants (+), plus our works (50), equals (=) Salvation

The key to the equation is the plus symbol, or the covenant. That is what joins us with Jesus and gives us access to His perfect saving power and attributes. It is similar to a marriage, where we join our lives with our spouse, take upon us the same last name, and have access to each other's abilities and talents. That is why in the scriptures the covenant between us and Jesus is so often likened to marriage (see Hosea 1; Isaiah 62:5).

Here is one example from author Anthony Sweat of the importance of taking a name in marriage.

> One of the ways I knew for a fact that my wife *truly* loved me was that she was willing to take upon her the last name of "Sweat." Ladies, of all the names in the world you might take upon yourself in marriage, did you ever consider yours might be a body function? I am sure my wife didn't either.
>
> Nevertheless, when she went to have her name officially changed to Sweat, the government official looked at her and said, "Are you really sure you want to do this?" To which she said, "Yes."
>
> Oh, true love! When a girl is willing to become known as Mrs. Sweat, you know it's eternal.

The beauty of the marriage covenant is that two people join their very lives together, becoming "one flesh" (Genesis 2:24) and one name (see Moses 6:9). When a man and a woman marry, they can share in each other's strengths, skills, and talents.

The same is true in our covenants with Christ. When we make a covenant with Him, we take upon us His name and give of our very lives to Him. In return, Jesus offers Himself to us—all of His virtues become our virtues, His goodness becomes our goodness, and His perfection becomes our perfection.

It is as simple as that: Take the name of Jesus upon us through the ordinance of baptism, enter into a covenant with Christ, and join our life with His. If we do that and remain faithful to our covenant, we will be saved by virtue of that covenant with Christ at the last day.

King Benjamin taught in the Book of Mormon,

> I would that ye should take upon you the name of Christ, all you that have entered into the covenant with God that ye should be obedient unto the end of your lives.
>
> And it shall come to pass that whosoever doeth this shall be found at the right hand of God, for he shall know the name by

which he is called; for he shall be called by the name of Christ. (Mosiah 5:8–9)

The Covenants of the Holy Temple

Being "saved" in the celestial kingdom is very different than being "exalted" in the celestial kingdom. To be saved means that we are blessed to live eternally in the celestial kingdom and in the presence of God. The covenant and ordinance of salvation is baptism. But being "exalted" means that not only do we live with God, but we can *become* like Him.

To be exalted, we need additional covenants beyond baptism, specifically the covenants and ordinances of the temple. *True to the Faith* teaches that "the principal purpose of temples is to provide the ordinances necessary for our exaltation in the celestial kingdom."[3] In the temple we participate in many covenants and ordinances. President Boyd K. Packer taught that we are "washed and anointed and instructed and endowed and sealed."[4]

Many of the covenants and ordinances in temples are related to families. In the temple a man and a woman may be sealed for time and all eternity and, with their children, form forever families, thus helping to fulfill one of the purposes of life. (See chapter 6.) Not only do we receive those ordinances for ourselves, but in the temple we can also perform gospel ordinances for those who have died without having received them. We "can be baptized and confirmed, receive the endowment, and participate in the sealings of husband to wife and children to parents."[5]

 Scan this QR code or visit http://www .youtube.com/watch?v=XLXYxmaHWQs to learn more about the blessings of temples.

What Covenants Do We Make in the Temple?

The following quotes explain the nature of some of the additional covenants we make in the temple:

- President Gordon B. Hinckley said that in the temple "we take upon ourselves covenants and obligations regarding lives of purity and virtue and goodness and truth and unselfishness to others."[6]
- The Church's booklet *Preparing to Enter the Holy Temple* says that "we covenant to give of our resources in time and money and talent—all we are and all we possess—to the interest of the kingdom of God upon the earth."[7]

The blessing of making additional covenants in the temple enables us to further join ourselves with the Savior. Elder David A. Bednar taught, "In the ordinances of the holy temple we more completely and fully take upon us the name of Jesus Christ."[8] Through temple covenants and ordinances, we can be washed, anointed, endowed, and sealed so we can fulfill our potential to become like our Heavenly Father and live in His eternal presence.

The Need to Make and Keep Covenants

If we take anything from the discussion in this chapter, it is this: one of the great tests of life is to make and keep covenants with Christ. President Boyd K. Packer taught, "Ordinances and covenants become our credentials for admission into [God's] presence. To worthily receive them is the quest of a lifetime; to keep them thereafter is the challenge of mortality."[9]

The great test of life isn't to be perfect, or not to make any mistakes. The only mistake we can really make in this life is to not make and keep covenants. We don't need to be perfect to go to heaven and become like God, we just need to be joined with Jesus, who will make us perfect. All of our efforts in living the gospel simply qualify us to make and keep covenants with Christ. Our faith and repentance—the first principles of the gospel—show that we are ready to make a covenant with God.

Elder D. Todd Christofferson said, "Our access to [God's] power is through our covenants with Him. . . . In these divine agreements, God binds himself to sustain, sanctify, and exalt us in return for our commitment to serve Him."[10] As you join yourself with Jesus through covenant and take His name upon you, we testify that Christ will "seal you his, that you may be brought to heaven, that ye may have everlasting salvation and eternal life" (Mosiah 5:15).

Blow up a balloon. Draw an X on a piece of paper and tape in on the wall across the room. Step back about ten feet. Now take your balloon, aim it, and try to hit the mark by releasing the balloon. Nice shootin', Tex. How did that work out for ya?

Now, thread a piece of string or fishing line through a straw and tape one end of the string to the X on the wall and the other end of the string to the other wall so the string is straight and tight. Then, blow up your balloon, tape it to the straw, and release it. Bam! Right on target.

Just like binding our balloon to the straw on a string put us on a straight course to our target, if we will bind our lives to Christ through covenant, He will point us on "a straight course to eternal bliss" (Alma 37:44) and make it possible to hit our mark of the celestial kingdom.

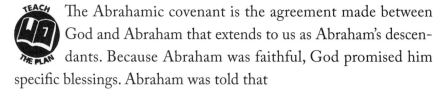

We invite you to make a covenant and join yourself with Jesus this week by partaking of the sacrament and renewing your baptismal covenant. Or, if you aren't a member of the Church, ponder on the scriptures about baptism discussed at the beginning of this chapter and learn more about the covenant of baptism by studying about it in the scriptures. (We recommend 2 Nephi 31 as a good place to start.)

Still Have Questions?

What is the Abrahamic covenant?

The Abrahamic covenant is the agreement made between God and Abraham that extends to us as Abraham's descendants. Because Abraham was faithful, God promised him specific blessings. Abraham was told that

- His posterity would be numerous (see Genesis 17:5–6; Abraham 2:9; 3:14).
- His seed, or descendants, would receive the gospel and bear the priesthood (see Abraham 2:9).
- Through the ministry of his seed, "all the families of the earth [would] be blessed, even with the blessings of the Gospel, which are the blessings of salvation, even of life eternal" (Abraham 2:11).[11]

We can summarize and remember the Abrahamic covenant with the following "three Ps"—priesthood, posterity, and promised land.

1. *Priesthood.* Abraham and his descendants were promised that they would have the priesthood and would thus be responsible to take the gospel to all the nations of the earth.

2. *Posterity.* Abraham was promised that he would have a

countless, eternal posterity. Those who remain faithful to the Abrahamic covenant receive this same promise of having an eternal family and posterity, which is made possible through the blessings of temple marriage.

3. *Promised land.* Abraham was promised a specific geographical area in the Middle East. This "promised land" also can be thought of as referring to the celestial kingdom, which those who are faithful to the Abrahamic covenant will inherit.

In return for these blessings, Abraham promised that his family would take the gospel and its priesthood ordinances to all the earth (see Abraham 2:9–11). As the covenant children of Abraham and as part of the house of Israel, we receive the same promised blessings as Abraham did as we fulfill our end of the covenant to bless the whole world with the blessings of the gospel.

Will my good works get me into heaven?

Some people—even some Latter-day Saints—get confused and mistakenly think that it is only our good works that will save us in the celestial kingdom. If we can only pay enough tithing, go to enough church meetings, set up 100,000 metal chairs, and serve enough people, then we will be qualified for heaven! Wrong. Those good works are wonderful—but they won't save us. Our good works contribute to our salvation in the sense that they act as prerequisites for making covenants with God. It's like making a sports team. Our good works are like the tryout, but it's making and being a part of the Savior's team that enables us to win the game of salvation.

Teach the Plan!

Connected to Christ by Covenants

Objective: To help learners understand the importance of making and keeping covenants.

Attention Getter: Give your children the quiz next to Teach the Plan #1. After hearing their answers, share with them the Savior's list next to Teach the Plan #2.

Visual: Show your children the covenant contract next to Teach the Plan #3. Ask, "What are the terms of the baptismal covenant?"

Analogy: Share with your children the math analogy next to Teach the Plan #4. Ask, "How is the Savior's Atonement like the number infinity?"

Lesson Activity: Share Anthony Sweat's story next to Teach the Plan #5. Ask, "What does it mean to take upon us the name of Christ? How does this relate to becoming the children of Christ?" Then read Mosiah 5:7.

Visual: Watch the video linked at Teach the Plan #6.

Lesson Activity: Teach the Plan #7: Help your children understand what the Abrahamic covenant is and what it means for them. Encourage them to memorize the "three Ps" of the covenant. Discuss how those "three Ps" apply to them as children of Abraham.

Activity: Do the Experiment upon the Word activity with the balloon and straw. Use this activity to lead a discussion with your family about how binding ourselves to God through covenant puts us on the path to eternal life.

Invitation to Act: Invite your children to accept the Live the Plan invitation to learn more about the baptismal covenant.

10

Being Born . . . Again

Transformers are cool. Whoever thought up the idea was a genius. Wouldn't it be great to *be* a Transformer, and change from one thing to another? We just want to say that you, Mr. Transformer-inventor, simply rock.

While there are some sweet *toy* Transformers out there, we're actually talking about *real* transformations. And the "inventor" of our true transformation is *The Rock*—Jesus Christ.

The Savior said, "All mankind, yea, men and women, all nations, kindreds, tongues and people, *must be born again*; yea, born of God, *changed* from their carnal and fallen state, to a state of righteousness, being redeemed of God, becoming his sons and daughters; and thus they become new creatures; and unless they do this, they can in nowise inherit the kingdom of God" (Mosiah 27:25–26; emphasis added).

Sometimes we read about being "born again" in the scriptures and wonder what it means. Sometimes we hear about it and think that being "born again" is just a mainstream Christian thing and that Mormons don't believe in it. Actually, being "born again" is one of the most important things that Mormons *do* believe in, and it is fundamental to the doctrine of the plan of salvation and central to our purpose here on earth.

Elder Dallin H. Oaks said, "As we understand these scriptures, our answer to whether we have been born again is clearly 'yes.' We were born again when we entered into a covenant relationship with our Savior by being born of water and of the Spirit and by taking upon us the name of Jesus Christ."[1]

Being born again means changing—"transforming"—ourselves and our natures through the Atonement of Christ into new people who are like Jesus Christ and God the Father.

What Does It Mean to Be Born Again?

Jesus once taught a man named Nicodemus that "Except a man be born again, he cannot see the kingdom of God" (John 3:3). Nicodemus was confused; he was a grown man and thought the Savior was saying he needed to be *literally* born again.

Luckily for Nicodemus and for us, Jesus clarified the metaphor: "Except a man be born of water and of the Spirit, he cannot enter into the kingdom of God. . . . Marvel not that I said unto thee, Ye must be born again" (John 3:5, 7). Being born again is a metaphor connected to our first birth. When we come into this world as newborn babies, there isn't just a lot of crying—there is also a lot of blood and water (amniotic fluid) and a new spirit that enters this world.

Those same elements—blood, water, and spirit—are also necessary for our second birth—our *spiritual* birth. The Lord taught Adam, "Inasmuch as ye were born into the world by water, and blood, and the spirit, which I have made, and so became of dust a living soul, even so ye must be born again into the kingdom of heaven, of water, and of the Spirit, and be cleansed by blood, even the blood of mine Only Begotten" (Moses 6:59).

Although it is symbolic, being born again is a very real thing, and involves a very real change in our natures. Elder David A. Bednar said that being born again is "a spiritual rebirth and fundamental change of what we feel and desire, what we think and do, and what we are."[2] Being spiritually born again requires the Spirit of God to change our very natures.

Conversion: A Lifelong Process

 Sometimes the scriptures use the word "conversion" in place of being born again. Don't confuse this with when you hear people say they were "converted" to the Church by the missionaries and baptized. True conversion requires deep change and is not an event, but a process that takes place over time.

For example, the Apostle Peter was already a member of the Church and one of Christ's apostles. Peter had a powerful testimony of Jesus (see Matthew 16:15–16) and was chosen to be the leader of the Church after Christ was resurrected. Yet, Jesus said to Peter, "When thou art converted, strengthen thy brethren" (Luke 22:32), implying that Peter was still in the process of changing and becoming the person he needed to become—that Peter wasn't yet fully converted.

Being converted (or born again) is a lifelong process of overcoming the desires of the natural man and conquering them in order to become the spiritual person God wants us to be.

Transform the following fractions into decimals:

A. ⅓

B. ⅕

C. ⅛

D. ²⁄₉

E. ³⁄₁₀

The way you transform a fraction into a decimal is by dividing the top number of the fraction (the numerator) by the bottom number of the fraction (the denominator), like this:

$2/9 = 2 \div 9 = .22$

How is this like being transformed into a born-again believer in the Savior? How is it different?

(Answers: A. 0.33, B. 0.20, C: 0.125, D. 0.22, E. 0.30)

What Does God Want Us to Change?

 We are God's spirit children, and He loves us. Each soul has great worth in His sight (see Doctrine and Covenants 18:10) because we are His offspring (see Romans 8:16). Inside of each of us is the ability to become like God. But to reach our divine potential, we must overcome the "natural man" that is inside each of us as mortals.

The feelings inside each of us and the parts of our character that are not consistent with the gospel of Jesus Christ and His divine attributes are known as the "natural man." Our natural man wants to be selfish, lazy, mean, stubborn, prideful, and immoral. It wants to cheat, lie, steal, hurt, and destroy.

However, inside each of us is a spiritual person as well—one who wants to conquer the natural man, change our bad attributes, and become like Christ. Almost daily, a battle takes place between our fallen natures and our spiritual natures—our natural man and our Christlike man.

We read in the Book of Mormon that "the natural man is an enemy to God, and has been from the fall of Adam, and will be, forever and ever, unless he yields to the enticings of the Holy Spirit, and putteth off the natural man and becometh a saint through the atonement of Christ the Lord, and becometh as a child, submissive, meek, humble, patient, full of love, willing to submit to all things which the Lord seeth fit to inflict upon him, even as a child doth submit to his father" (Mosiah 3:19).

We can choose either to be led by our carnal or "evil nature" (Enos 1:20), or we can become "partakers of the divine nature" (2 Peter 1:4) by using the Atonement of Jesus Christ to change the things in us that aren't like God and becoming born again.

What Does the Holy Ghost Have to Do with Being Born Again?

One of the roles of the Holy Ghost is to sanctify us, or make us pure and holy. Elder Bruce R. McConkie taught that "the Holy Ghost is the *Sanctifier*. It is through his power . . . that men may be sanctified and washed clean from all sin."[3] Each time we receive the Holy Ghost, his influence purifies us, influences us, and changes us bit by bit. That is one reason why we are commanded to be baptized and receive the Holy Ghost (see Doctrine and Covenants 35:6): without receiving the Holy Ghost, we cannot receive the Atonement of Jesus Christ and be changed. Our natural man is changed and converted when we receive the Holy Ghost and yield "to the enticings of the Holy Spirit" (Mosiah 3:19).

Receiving the Holy Ghost requires a steady succession of gospel actions, covenants, and ordinances. Covenants are the key to receiving the Holy Ghost and being changed through its reception. King Benjamin taught, "Because of the *covenant* which ye have made ye shall be called the children of Christ, his sons, and his daughters; for behold, this day he hath spiritually begotten you; for ye say that your hearts are changed through faith on his name; therefore, ye are born of him and have become his sons and his daughters" (Mosiah 5:7; emphasis added).

Each time we participate in gospel covenants and ordinances—such as baptism, the sacrament, and the temple—we are able to receive the Holy Ghost that we may "always have his Spirit to be with [us]" (Moroni 4:3). As we receive the Spirit, it changes us. Thus, to be born again we need to be continually participating in the "righteous cycle" of faith, repentance, making covenants, receiving the Holy Ghost, and being sanctified by its reception—being changed, little by little. Each time we participate in this process, we become more and more like Christ and our natural man is converted into a spiritual man, helping us to be born again.

 Spend one day doing everything you can possibly do to invite the Holy Ghost to be with you. How did you feel at the end of the day? How would your life be different if you did this every day?

What Is the Righteous Cycle?

The righteous cycle is opposite of the "pride cycle." It is the cycle that leads us *toward* becoming like Christ. Below is an example of the "righteous cycle":

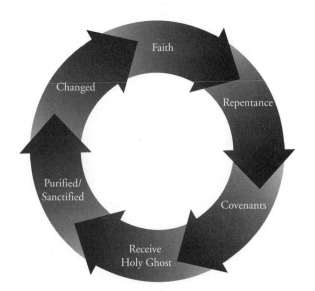

As we go through this righteous cycle, we are not only purified and sanctified by the Holy Ghost, but we are also eventually *changed* to become like Christ. The ultimate purpose of the "righteous cycle" is to connect us to Christ through covenants and to help us *become* like Christ through the infinite Atonement and the cleansing power of the Holy Ghost. Elder Dallin H. Oaks said, "The gospel of Jesus Christ is the plan by which we can become what children of God are supposed to become. This spotless and perfected state will result from a *steady succession* of covenants, ordinances, and actions."[4]

Elder David A. Bednar likened our spiritual conversion to the process that turns a cucumber into a pickle. He said, "A cucumber becomes a pickle as it is prepared and cleaned, immersed in and saturated with salt brine, and sealed in a sterilized container. This procedure requires time and cannot be hurried, and none of the essential steps can be ignored or avoided." Similarly, "total immersion in and saturation with the Savior's gospel are essential steps in the process of being born again."[5] We can't just dip ourselves once or twice—going to church here and there, reading the scriptures now and then, praying off and on—and expect to become spiritual pickles! It takes total and steady immersion to change our very natures!

Conversion Is a Process, Not a Checklist

It is important to emphasize that spiritual rebirth isn't about a checklist of outward ordinances; it's about what is happening *inside* of us—what is happening to our hearts and our natures. Sometimes we think the gospel is a one big checklist of things to do: go to Church, read the scriptures, say our prayers, serve others, pay tithing, etc. It is easy to fall into a robotic routine and focus on the outward action and not the inward purpose.

While the gospel *actions* are important, what is more important is what those actions do to us on the inside. If we do those actions with the right intent and purpose, then those actions will help us receive the Holy Ghost and help convert and change us. If not, then the Spirit cannot enter our heart and help us be changed and born again.

In addition, it's not up to other people to convert us. Our

parents, leaders, teachers, and friends can help us in coming unto Christ and being converted, but ultimately whether we are converted or not is totally between us and the Lord, and no one else. *True to the Faith* teaches: "You have primary responsibility for your own conversion. No one can be converted for you, and no one can force you to be converted."[6] Conversion is a matter of you exercising your agency by making and keeping sacred covenants. You can do it!

Is a "Testimony" Enough?

Sometimes we focus a lot in church meetings on gaining a "testimony" and believing in the Church. While a testimony is necessary, it is actually not the end result we are trying to accomplish. After all, have you ever considered that Satan also believes that Joseph Smith is a prophet (which is why he tried to stop Joseph from praying in the grove), that the Book of Mormon is true (which is why he tries to stop us from reading it), and that the Church is true (which is why he tries to stop us from going).

The Apostle James said, "Thou believest that there is one God; thou doest well: the devils also believe, and tremble" (James 2:19). Believing something is not enough—we must become something because of what we believe. That's one of the devil's problems: he isn't *converted* by what he knows to be true because he doesn't live it.

Elder Dallin H. Oaks taught: "It is not even enough for us to be *convinced* of the gospel; we must act and think so that we are *converted* by it. In contrast to the institutions of the world, which teach us to *know* something, the gospel of Jesus Christ challenges us to *become* something."[7]

Let's not only believe . . . let's have our beliefs change us to become Christlike people.

What If I'm Not Becoming Born Again Fast Enough?

At times we can become frustrated because we don't feel like we are becoming converted quickly enough. Although our first birth was finished within nine months, our second birth of being born again and converted spiritually will take a lifetime—and probably well into the next one. Don't become discouraged. Remember, "Conversion is a process, not an event. . . . It is a quiet miracle. . . . Because conversion is a quiet, constant process, you may be converted now and not realize it."[8]

Tall people didn't become tall overnight. Accomplished artists didn't learn to paint in a day. Physical muscles aren't built by lifting one weight in a single workout. And spiritually converted people didn't become like Christ in an instant. President Ezra Taft Benson taught:

> We must be careful, as we seek to become more and more godlike, that we do not become discouraged and lose hope. Becoming Christlike is a lifetime pursuit and very often involves growth and change that is slow, almost imperceptible. The scriptures record remarkable accounts of men whose lives changed dramatically, in an instant, as it were. . . .
>
> But we must be cautious as we discuss these remarkable examples. Though they are real and powerful, they are the exception more than the rule. For every Paul, for every Enos, and for every King Lamoni, there are hundreds and thousands of people who find the process of repentance much more subtle, much more imperceptible. Day by day they move closer to the Lord, little realizing they are building a godlike life. They live quiet lives of goodness, service, and commitment.[9]

And Elder D. Todd Christofferson taught, "You may ask, Why doesn't this mighty change happen more quickly with me? You should remember that the remarkable examples of King Benjamin's people, Alma, and some others in scripture are just that—remarkable and not typical. For most of us, the changes are more gradual and occur over time. Being born again, unlike our physical birth, is more a process than an event."[10]

We can continue to transform our very natures on a daily basis. As we seek to receive the Holy Ghost through living the righteous cycle of faith, repenting, making and keeping covenants, and being obedient, we will conquer our natural man little by little. As Alma taught, we each need to be "spiritually . . . born of God," having "received his image in [our] countenances," and experiencing a "mighty change of heart" (Alma 5:14).

That is what being born again is. That is what conversion is. When we die and face the Lord at the Judgment, He will want to see what we have *become*. (See chapter 17.) He will want to see if we are still a natural man, or if we have become a spiritual man, born not only once physically, but born again spiritually.

We testify of the reality and divinity of a living Savior who invites us to come unto Him and "be ye *transformed*" (Romans 12:2; emphasis added).

Still Have Questions?

What if I don't think I can change my nature? What if that is just who I am, and I can't become Christlike?

The world teaches that our natural desires control us, affecting how we act and who we become. We testify that God has given each of us agency—the power of *independent* action—and *we* can control how we act and who we become. We testify that the Atonement of Jesus Christ can give us strength to resist temptation (see 1 Corinthians 10:13); it has the power to convert our very natures.

President George Q. Cannon explained:

> If any of us are imperfect, it is our duty to pray for the gift that will make us perfect. . . . If I am an angry man, it is my duty to pray for charity, which suffereth long and is kind. . . . So with all the gifts of the Gospel. They are intended for this purpose. No man ought to say, 'Oh, I cannot help this; it is my nature.' He is not justified in it, for the reason that God has promised to give strength to correct these things, and to give gifts that will eradicate them.[11]

Why are trials necessary to transform us?

Did you know that coal (graphite) and diamonds are primarily both made of carbon—just arranged differently? Coal can be turned into a diamond through a process of heat and high pressure that causes the carbon atoms to release and be reordered into a stacked pyramid that forms a diamond.[12] (And you thought your Christmas present last year was useless. Ha, thank Santa for that potential diamond!)

The tests and trials we face in this life—the heat and high pressure so to speak—also have the potential to change and convert us into becoming more like Christ. If we will be humble and let the Lord reorder our lives through test and trial, He can also turn the coal of our natural man into the diamond that reflects His image in our countenance (see Alma 5:14).

Teach the Plan!

Being Born . . . Again

Objective: To help learners understand what it means to be born again and how to help the process of spiritual rebirth happen in their lives.

Attention Getter: If you have any Transformers toys, bring one to the lesson and ask one of your kids to transform it as quickly as possible. Then share the section on toy Transformers versus true transformation next to Teach the Plan #1.

Discussion Question: Ask your children, "What does it mean to be born again?" After listening to their answers, share the material found in Teach the Plan #2.

Quotation and Discussion Question: Read the quotation from Elder David A. Bednar next to Teach the Plan #3. Ask, "Based on this definition, do you think you have been born again?" (Note, there are sometimes questions about a person's level of conversion if he or she has never had some kind of huge spiritual experience. This issue is addressed at Teach the Plan #4).

Activity: Have your children do the Experiment upon the Word activity. Ask, "How can we connect this kind of transformation with the transformation of spiritual rebirth?"

Discussion Question: Ask your children, "What does God want us to change?" After listening to their answers, share the material found in Teach the Plan #5.

Discussion Question: Ask your children, "What does the Holy Ghost have to do with being born again?" After listening to their answers, share the material found in Teach the Plan #6.

Visual: Show your children the cyclical chart that goes along with Teach the Plan #7. Point out that getting into a "righteous cycle" will help increase our conversion.

Discussion Question: Ask your children, "What is the difference between being converted to the gospel and just believing in it? After they share their responses, share with them the paragraphs that go along with Teach the Plan #9.

Visual: Show a picture of a cucumber and a pickle (or, bring samples of the food to taste). Share Elder David A. Bednar's quote at Teach the Plan #8. Ask

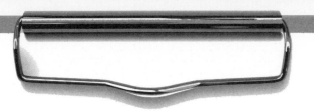

your children, "How can we more fully immerse ourselves in the gospel of Jesus Christ?"

Making It Personal: There are several relevant questions discussed in this chapter (see Teach the Plan #10, 11, and 12). Select the questions that would be most beneficial for your children and discuss them together.

Invitation to Act: Invite your children to accept the invitation next to the Live the Plan icon and encourage them to record their experience in their journal.

11

The Family: It's about . . . Eternity

Think of the greatest love story ever—the two people who just defined the happiness that comes from true, eternal love. Got it?

Were you thinking of Romeo and Juliet? Maybe Cleopatra and Mark Antony? Or Wesley and Princess Buttercup? What about Shrek and Fiona?

Well, we hate to break it to all you hopeless romantics, but while each of those stories (or whichever one you thought of) might be a great love story, they don't even come close to the *greatest* love story ever. The greatest love story ever is your parents' story. ("Ew, gross!")

No, not your earthly parents—we're talking about your Heavenly Parents.

When we were in the premortal existence (see chapter 1), we experienced for ourselves what it was like to live in a heavenly family, being completely loved and wonderfully taught as children in the family of God. We had heavenly parents who were full of complete happiness, and who showed us the joy that comes from having an eternal marriage and an eternal family.

Imagine our excitement when our Heavenly Father told us of His eternal plan of salvation and said that if we would follow the plan we could become like Him and eventually have—for ourselves—an eternal marriage and family of our very own!

And now we are here on earth, trying to create that future eternal family for ourselves. To guide us in developing our own eternal families, the First Presidency and Quorum of the Twelve Apostles issued "The Family: A Proclamation to the World."[1] Here are eight fundamental statements from that document that relate to the purpose of the family in the plan of salvation, and to our role in helping to create an eternal family.

"Ordained of God"

"Marriage between a man and a woman is ordained of God and . . . the family is central to the Creator's plan for the eternal destiny of His children."

The Lord doesn't focus on the family just because it is cute, or sentimental, or good for society (although it is all of those things). No, the Lord focuses on the family because without an eternal marriage we cannot become exalted or be like God (see Doctrine and Covenants 131:1–4; 132:19–20).

Also, "God has established families to bring happiness to His children, allow them to learn correct principles in a loving atmosphere, and prepare them for eternal life. The home is the best place to teach, learn, and apply gospel principles."[2] The family is the organization of God, and it is the most efficient and effective way to fulfill God's plan to help us progress and learn to become more like Him.

"United Eternally"

"The divine plan of happiness enables family relationships to be perpetuated beyond the grave. Sacred ordinances and covenants available in holy temples make it possible for individuals to return to the presence of God and for families to be united eternally."

Through the Prophet Joseph Smith, God revealed that our families can be together forever. When a man and a woman are sealed in the temple, they create an eternal marriage. This means that the husband and wife can remain married throughout all eternity, and the children who are born to them (or later sealed to them) will be a part of their eternal family also.

The single most important thing we can do or will ever do in this life is, as Elder Bruce R. McConkie said, "to marry the right person in the right place by the right authority" in the temple.[3]

Author John Hilton shared this story:

> On my mission, my companion and I were teaching Paul and Charlene. They were a young couple and full of love for each other. They were especially excited when we taught them about eternal families. However, there were some parts of the gospel that were hard for them to live, and they ultimately decided that they did not want to be a part of the Church.
>
> At our last discussion, Charlene said, "I understand what you taught about eternal marriage, but our love is so strong that we will be together forever. God won't be able to separate us."
>
> What she said was touching, beautiful, and *false*. In fact, God has specifically said the opposite: "Therefore, if a man marry him a wife in the world, and he marry her not by me nor by my word, and he covenant with her so long as he is in the world and she with him, their covenant and marriage are not of force when they are dead, and when they are out of the world; therefore, they are not bound by any law when they are out of the world" (Doctrine and Covenants 132:15).
>
> My companion and I shared that verse with Paul and Charlene, but they had made their decision. As we left their home, I felt so sad that they didn't seem to understand that if you are not sealed in the temple, no matter how much you love each other, you will not be together forever with your spouse.

Find the matching fingerprints below:

Just like you were focused on finding the match to the fingerprints, our lives should be focused on finding an eternal "match" and being sealed in the temple. President David O. McKay, quoting J. E. McCulloch, said that "no other success can compensate for failure in the home."[4] What this means is that creating a successful marriage and family means more for our salvation than any other accomplishment in our life, no matter how great it may be.

"Multiply and Replenish"

"We declare that God's commandment for His children to multiply and replenish the earth remains in force."

Many of the messages of the world today are antimarriage and antifamily: Wait longer and longer to get married and have fewer and fewer children. Or, don't get married at all and don't have any children at all.

However, if we are here on earth to become more like our heavenly parents, then part of the plan of salvation is for us to one day become earthly parents. Since the purpose of life is fulfilled through eternal marriage and family, then anything that is antimarriage and antifamily is anti-God's plan of salvation. As General Relief Society President Julie B. Beck taught, "Any doctrine or principle our youth hear from the world that is antifamily is also anti-Christ. It's that clear."[5]

"Powers of Procreation"

"God has commanded that the sacred powers of procreation are to be employed only between man and woman, lawfully wedded as husband and wife."

One of the first things we need to understand about this is that sex between a husband and wife is a *good* thing, not a bad one (Yes, that's right! We believe sex is a good thing—at the right time).

For the Strength of Youth teaches: "Physical intimacy between husband and wife is beautiful and sacred. It is ordained of God for the creation of children and for the expression of love between husband and wife. God has commanded that sexual intimacy be reserved for marriage."[6]

Sex in marriage is good because it brings children into married families and is a way to express love and commitment between husband and wife. However, when sex happens between unmarried people, God disapproves of it. Premarital sex can lead to premarital pregnancy, single parenthood, abortion, adultery, divorce, mistrust, guilt, and sexually transmitted diseases.

 Scan this QR code or visit https://lds .org/youth/video/chastity-what-are-the -limits to watch a video that can help answer questions about sexual purity.

"Love and Care for Each Other"

"Husband and wife have a solemn responsibility to love and care for each other and for their children."

Since we are here to learn to become more like God, learning to love is essential. The scriptures teach us that "he that loveth not knoweth not God; for God is love" (1 John 4:8). In the family setting, we are able to develop the Godlike attribute of charity and love towards other people because we are always around them. Showing love to our family helps us have eternal families. The following experience about how Joseph Smith showed love to his wife is recounted by a man named Jesse Crosby.

Brother Crosby lived in Nauvoo with Joseph Smith, and one day

Joseph brought a sack of flour to the Crosbys' house. Brother Crosby felt that it was inappropriate for Joseph to be carrying around flour because of the many important duties Joseph had.

Jesse said to Joseph that carrying flour was

> "too terrible a humiliation. . . . for you who are the head [of the house], and you should not do it."
>
> "The Prophet listened quietly to all he had to say, then made answer in these words: 'If there be humiliation in a man's house, who but the head of that house should or could bear that humiliation?' . . .
>
> ". . . If a man cannot learn in this life to appreciate a wife and do his duty by her, in properly taking care of her, he need not expect to be given one in the hereafter."[7]

Young men, be the kind of husband that your wife will want to stay married to in the next life.

"Essential to His Eternal Plan"

"Marriage between man and woman is essential to His eternal plan."

In the Doctrine and Covenants, we learn that were it not for the "sealing of [families] the whole earth [would] be smitten with a curse and *utterly wasted at his coming*" (Doctrine and Covenants 138:48; emphasis added). A primary purpose of our coming to earth is to form eternal families. If there were no temples and no eternal families, the creation of the entire earth would have been a waste, as without eternal families we cannot become like God.

Some people think that marriage is too hard, that the opposite sex is too complicated, and that perhaps it is better to remain single. However, Elder David A. Bednar explained why men and women need each other in marriage: "By divine design, men and women are intended to progress together toward perfection and a fulness of glory. Because of their distinctive temperaments and capacities, males and females each bring to a marriage relationship unique perspectives and experiences. The man and the woman contribute differently but equally to a oneness and a unity that can be achieved in no other way."[8]

"Founded upon the Teachings of the Lord Jesus Christ"

"Happiness in family life is most likely to be achieved when founded upon the teachings of the Lord Jesus Christ."

Think of how successful our families would be if, as parents and children, we applied Jesus' teachings of kindness, compassion, selflessness, love, forgiveness, respect, obedience, and honor. Whether we are the parents or the children, we can all do our part to help build a happy home.

For the Strength of Youth teaches:

> Be cheerful, helpful, and considerate of family members. Many problems in the home come from family members speaking and acting selfishly or unkindly. Seek to be a peacemaker rather than to tease, fight, and quarrel. Show love for your family members each day. Share your testimony with your family through words and actions. Your righteous example can make a difference in strengthening your family.
>
> Honor your parents by showing love and respect for them. Obey them as they lead you in righteousness. Willingly help in your home. Participate in wholesome family activities and traditions. Join your family in family prayer, family scripture study, and family home evenings.[9]

As we talk with people in their twenties and thirties, we frequently hear a similar story: "In high school I spent a lot of time with my friends, and we said we would always be friends—but I haven't seen them for years. I talk with my family members every week though."

 Sometimes it seems that spending time with our siblings and parents isn't very important, and that it isn't as much fun as being with our friends. However, we aren't sealed to our friends! Perhaps that is why President Ezra Taft Benson said, "Your most important friendships should be with your own brothers and sisters and with your father and mother."[10] As we do love and serve our family, we help foster an environment for our current family to become a celestial family.

Scan this QR code or visit http://www .lds.org/youth/video/two-brothers-apart to watch a video clip about two brothers and how they chose to become best friends.

Do something nice for one of your family members. It might be supporting them at a school event, writing them a note of love or appreciation, or helping a younger sibling with a problem they are having. You can make a huge difference in the lives of your family members. Now go do it!

"Individual Adaptation"

"Disability, death, or other circumstances may necessitate individual adaptation."

We know that there are many who are reading this book who—through no fault of their own—come from dysfunctional, broken, or single-parent homes. Please understand that you are loved and valued by God. After all, many great people—prophets included—have come from broken, dysfunctional, nonmember, or single-parent families. (For example, read Abraham 1 where Abraham's apostate dad tried to have him killed!) God loves *all* His children.

Regarding the family, it is important to understand that God first teaches us the ideal we should strive for, and then allows us to adapt depending on our circumstances.

Elder Richard G. Scott defined the ideal, eternal family this way: "Through the restored gospel we learn there is an *ideal family*. It is a family composed of a righteous Melchizedek Priesthood bearer with a righteous wife sealed to him and children born in the covenant or sealed to them."[11]

Because of situations that may be beyond your control, the family you are in right now might not be ideal. However, if we are faithful and do our part, all the blessings of an eternal family will be given to us, whether in this life or the next. We are promised that those "whose circumstances do not allow them to receive the blessings of eternal marriage and parenthood in this life will receive all promised blessings in the eternities, provided they keep the covenants they have made with God."[12]

The Ultimate Purpose

We conclude with a quote from President Boyd K. Packer, "The ultimate purpose of every teaching, every activity in the Church is that parents and their children are happy at home, sealed in an eternal marriage, and linked to their generations."[13] We testify that the purpose of life is facilitated and fulfilled in marriage and the family.

Still Have Questions?

What does the Church teach about divorce?

As we discuss the doctrine of eternal families, we know that some families have parents who are divorced. We obviously cannot judge others' situations, however, as a general rule, the Church disapproves of divorce, calling it a "plague" coming from the "work of the adversary."[14]

Speaking of marriage, Jesus said, "What therefore God hath joined together, let not man put asunder" (Matthew 19:6). When the Pharisees questioned this position, saying that Moses allowed divorce, Jesus answered, "Moses because of the hardness of your hearts suffered you to put away your wives: but from the beginning it was not so" (Matthew 19:8).

True to the Faith teaches that, as a rule, "the remedy for most marriage stress is not in divorce or separation. The remedy is found in the gospel of Jesus Christ—in repentance, forgiveness, integrity, and love. It is found in treating your spouse as you would like to be treated."[15]

What happens if my parents are divorced, then they both remarry and are sealed to other people? Who will I be sealed to in the next life?

These kind of questions can be complicated, and we know that there can be a lot of hurt behind questions like these. To those who are concerned about who they will be sealed to in the next life, all we know is that in the celestial kingdom everything will be perfectly fair, just, right, and good, and we will have a fullness of joy. The scriptures teach that "God shall wipe away all tears from their eyes; and there shall be no more death, neither sorrow, nor crying, neither shall there be any more pain: for the former things are passed away" (Revelation 21:4).

Elder Dallin H. Oaks said, "Singleness, childlessness, death, and divorce frustrate ideals and postpone the fulfillment of promised blessings. . . . But these frustrations are only temporary. The Lord has promised that in the eternities no blessing will be denied his sons and daughters who keep the commandments . . . and desire what is right."[16] God will ensure that all eternal family relationships will be worked out fairly.

What does the Lord teach about same-gender marriage?

Anything that is inconsistent with God's plan of salvation for His children is not endorsed by the Lord. We are all the spirit children of "heavenly parents"[17]—an eternal *Father and Mother* in heaven—and the primary purpose of God's plan for us is to become more like them. Therefore, The Church of Jesus Christ of Latter-day Saints "affirms that marriage between a man and a woman is essential to the Creator's plan for the eternal destiny of His children."[18] A same-gender marriage is inconsistent with the doctrine on eternal marriage and its purpose, and it is inconsistent with the teachings of the purposes of human sexuality, which are closely tied to the biological powers and responsibilities of creating and raising children. Therefore, the Church does not sanction or support same-gender marriages, and "affirms defining marriage as the legal and lawful union between a man and a woman."[19]

My parents were sealed, but later my dad treated my mom terribly and they got divorced. If they never re-marry, will they still be sealed in the next life?

It's important to realize that being sealed in the temple does not guarantee that a husband and wife will be together forever. They both have to honor the temple covenants they made. Elder Richard G. Scott said, "I don't believe that the temple ordinance guarantees that we'll be together forever. There will be a time before that sealing of the Holy Spirit of Promise makes it eternal where we'll be in the presence of the Savior, as individuals, and there will be a choice whether we continue with the sealing or not. And I want to do everything in my power to qualify so that she'll choose for that sealing to be eternal."[20]

Teach the Plan!

The Family: It's about . . . Eternity

Objective: To help deepen learners' understanding that the family is the central unit of God's plan of happiness and is necessary for exaltation.

Attention Getter: Ask one of your children to tell the group the most important decision he or she made that day. Then ask someone else to tell about the most important decision they made this past week. Then the past month. Then the past year. Then ask, "What do you think the most important decision you will ever make in your life will be?" Read the quote from Elder Bruce R. McConkie next to Teach the Plan #2 for the answer.

Activity: Do the Experiment upon the Word activity and match the fingerprints. Discuss why finding your eternal match and creating an eternal family should be the greatest focus of our lives.

Quotation and Discussion Question: Ask your family what the point is of each of the following activities: What is the point of today's seminary class? Last week's Mutual? Sunday's lesson? Last year's youth conference? Today's family home evening? After each answer, smile and say, "Nope." Then read President Boyd K. Packer's quote next to Teach the Plan #8 and discuss what the point truly is of every church activity and why that is true.

Lesson Activity: Teach the Plan #1. Write each of the following words on slips of paper and put them in a bowl: "1: Central," "2: Temples," "3: Multiply," "4: Powers," "5: Love," "6: Essential," "7: Happiness," "8: Adaptation." Have each child draw out one word (or more if you wish) and read the section from the book relating to one of the eight quotes from the family proclamation that it corresponds to. (Go to http://seek.deseretbook.com/bigpicture to download a handout of each of the eight sections from the family proclamation on its own page.) Have each person explain what their word teaches them about the family and how it applies to their family situation right now.

Lesson Activity: Teach the Plan #6. Read President Ezra Taft Benson's quote and then ask each family member to do a "five-minute service" as an act of friendship and love for another family member. (Acts of service might include writing a quick note, cleaning something, reading a book to a younger sibling, etc.)

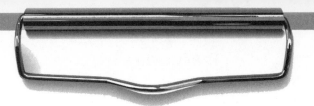

Have them report after five minutes about what they did and about how acts of service can develop love and friendship in a family. Then watch the video clip from Teach the Plan #7.

Discussion Questions: The following questions may help your children in understanding, identifying, and applying some gospel truths related to eternal families:

Teach the Plan #3: "Why do you think Sister Julie B. Beck said that any message that is antifamily is anti-Christ? In what ways have you seen the adversary try to break down the traditional family? What are some 'good' things that can get in the way of creating, forming, and maintaining happy families if we are not careful?"

Teach the Plan #5: "Why would this earth be 'utterly wasted' if we weren't able to seal families together for eternity? What does that teach you about how to not have your individual life be 'utterly wasted'?"

Video: Teach the Plan #4: This video uses whiteboard illustrations to discuss sexual purity. After watching the video, have your children discuss which illustration they liked best. Discuss with them how sexual purity is related to forming successful families now and in the future.

Invitation to Act: Invite your children to do the Live the Plan service activity and follow up with them the next week to find out what they did.

Christ's Return to Earth

Imagine it's a bright and sunny afternoon, and as you drive down the road with your parents you look up and notice that the sky looks different than normal. The clouds are luminescent, bright, and heavenly. Suddenly, without warning, the sky seemingly bursts open and the veil between heaven and earth is split. Trumpets start sounding from the sky, and you see above you the most glorious being your mind could ever conceive of descending out of heaven and touching down on earth—Jesus Christ in all His glory has just returned to earth to rule and reign as King of kings and Lord of lords. The power of His resurrected glory—like fire—is transfiguring some people and consuming others.

Do you get out of your car and run towards the event, or away from it? Do you step forward in joy at Christ's appearance, or run and seek to "enter into the rock, and hide thee in the dust, for the fear of the Lord and the glory of his majesty shall smite thee" (2 Nephi 12:10)? In essence, are you prepared for the Second Coming of Jesus Christ?

What Is the Second Coming of Christ?

After His death and resurrection in Jerusalem, Jesus reappeared to His disciples there and taught them for a short time. Then, while in the midst of His disciples, "[Jesus] was taken up; and a cloud received him out of their sight" (Acts 1:9). As the disciples looked up into heaven, two angels appeared and said, "Ye men of Galilee, why stand ye gazing up into heaven? this same Jesus, which is taken up from you into heaven, *shall so come in like manner as ye have seen him go into heaven*" (Acts 1:11; emphasis added). Since that day, the Saints have anxiously waited for the Lord to return to the earth to rule and reign in power over the whole earth. This is known as the "second coming" of Jesus Christ.

The Second Coming of Christ will be very different than the first coming of Christ. At His first coming, Jesus was "born of Mary" and came to earth as a child (Alma 7:10), with the purpose of teaching God's children and fulfilling the Atonement. At the Second Coming, the Lord will come out of "the clouds of heaven with power and great glory" (Matthew 24:30) to "take vengeance upon the wicked" (Doctrine and Covenants 29:17) and to cleanse the earth from sin. The Lord told Joseph Smith: "For behold, verily, verily, I say unto you, the time is soon at hand that I shall come in a cloud with power and great glory. And it shall be a great day at the time of my coming" (Doctrine and Covenants 34:7–8). Indeed it will be a great day. In fact, for the righteous, the return of Jesus Christ will be one of the best days on earth.

What Will Happen at the Second Coming?

The prophet Joel described the Second Coming as both "the *great* and the *terrible* day of the Lord" (Joel 2:31; emphasis added). How can a day be great for some, but terrible for others? Well, it is because of what will happen when Jesus comes—for the righteous it will be the greatest day, but for the wicked and rebellious it won't be so great (that could be the understatement of the century). The scriptures teach us that at the Second Coming "among the wicked, men shall lift up their voices and curse God and die" (Doctrine and Covenants 45:32) and that the rebellious sinners' "faces shall be as flames" (2 Nephi 23:8). The Lord said, "For behold, the day cometh that shall burn as an oven; and all the proud, yea, and all that do wickedly, shall be stubble; and the day that cometh shall burn them up" (3 Nephi 25:1).

However, the Lord also says that at the Second Coming, "unto you that fear my name, shall the Son of Righteousness arise with healing in his wings" (3 Nephi 25:2). "The Lord shall be in their midst, and his glory shall be upon them, and he will be their king and their lawgiver" (Doctrine and Covenants 45:59), and "the righteous shall be gathered out from among all nations, and shall come to Zion, singing with songs of everlasting joy" (Doctrine and Covenants 45:71). Sin will cease, because when Jesus comes again, "Satan shall be bound, that he shall have no place in the hearts of the children of men" (Doctrine and Covenants 45:55). Perhaps best of all, all our righteous loved ones who have died will be resurrected at the Second Coming of Christ (see Doctrine and Covenants 45:45) and we will be with them again. Healing, singing, joy, sinlessness, and seeing our past loved ones—that doesn't sound too bad, does it? Yes, for the righteous the Second Coming will be a joyous day indeed. It will be the best day.

As we think about the Second Coming, we should be encouraged and joyful. If we are prepared, it will be a marvelous day.

What Are the Signs of the Second Coming?

"And it shall come to pass that he that feareth me shall be looking forth for the great day of the Lord to come, even for the signs of the coming of the Son of Man" (Doctrine and Covenants 45:39). In His mercy, the Lord wants us to be ready and righteous for His coming, so He has given us "signs" to help us prepare and anticipate His glorious return.

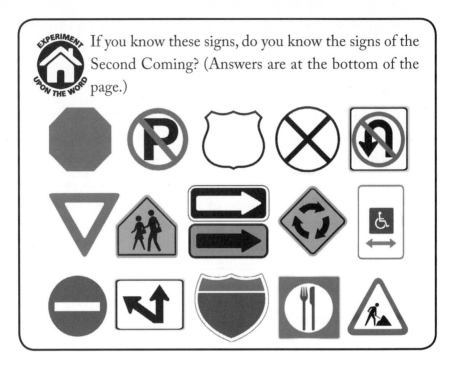

EXPERIMENT UPON THE WORD If you know these signs, do you know the signs of the Second Coming? (Answers are at the bottom of the page.)

TEACH 3 THE PLAN The following are *some* of the signs of the Second Coming listed in the scriptures (in no particular order). Some have been fulfilled, some are being fulfilled now, and some have yet to happen. As you go through the list, check off whether you think these signs are fulfilled, in process, or have yet to begin.

FULFILLED	IN PROCESS	NOT STARTED	
☐	☐	☐	Coming forth of the Book of Mormon (see Isaiah 29; Ezekiel 37; 2 Nephi 3, 27, 29)
☐	☐	☐	The gathering of Israel (see Isaiah 11:11–12; Doctrine and Covenants 45:25, 43)
☐	☐	☐	Wars and rumors of wars (see Matthew 24:6–7; Doctrine and Covenants 45:26)

(Answers: *Stop Sign, No Parking, State Highway, Railroad Crossing, No U-Turn, Yield, School Crossing, One Way/Detour, Circular Intersection, Reserved Handicapped Parking, Do Not Enter, Side Road, Interstate, Food, Workers Ahead*)

FULFILLED	IN PROCESS	NOT STARTED	
❑	❑	❑	The whole earth will be in commotion (see Doctrine and Covenants 45:26)
❑	❑	❑	People will despair in their hearts (see Doctrine and Covenants 45:26)
❑	❑	❑	Love of men will "wax cold" (see Matthew 24:12; Doctrine and Covenants 45:27)
❑	❑	❑	The Church will progress and fill the earth (see Daniel 2:34–35; 1 Nephi 14:12)
❑	❑	❑	The Lord will pour out His spirit upon all flesh. People will begin to have visions and dreams and prophesy (see Joel 2:28–32)
❑	❑	❑	False Christs and false prophets will appear and deceive people, including some members of the Church (see JS-Matthew 1:22; Matthew 24:24)
❑	❑	❑	People will reject the truth because of the philosophies of men (see Doctrine and Covenants 45:29)
❑	❑	❑	Widespread wickedness across the world (see Doctrine and Covenants 45:27; Matthew 24:37)
❑	❑	❑	The Gentiles will have great power and influence in the world (see Doctrine and Covenants 45:30; 1 Nephi 13:13–19)
❑	❑	❑	An overflowing scourge or desolating sickness shall cover the land (see Doctrine and Covenants 45:31)
❑	❑	❑	The righteous will be persecuted (see Matthew 24:9)
❑	❑	❑	The righteous will stand in holy places and come unto Zion for protection (see Doctrine and Covenants 45:32)
❑	❑	❑	People will curse God (see Doctrine and Covenants 45:32)
❑	❑	❑	There will be earthquakes in many places (see Isaiah 24:20; Matthew 24:7; Revelation 16:18–20; Doctrine and Covenants 45:33)
❑	❑	❑	There will be famines and pestilences (see Matthew 24:7)

FULFILLED	IN PROCESS	NOT STARTED	
☐	☐	☐	People will harden their hearts against God (see Doctrine and Covenants 45:33)
☐	☐	☐	Violence and murder will abound (see Doctrine and Covenants 45:33)
☐	☐	☐	Latter-day temples of the Lord will be built (see Isaiah 2:2; Isaiah 19:19–20; Micah 4:1–7)
☐	☐	☐	The sun will be darkened (see Joel 2:31; 3:15; Matthew 24:29; Doctrine and Covenants 45:42; 133:49)
☐	☐	☐	The moon will have the color of blood (see Matthew 24:29; Doctrine and Covenants 45:42; 133:49)
☐	☐	☐	Stars will fall from heaven (see Matthew 24:29; Doctrine and Covenants 45:42; 133:49)
☐	☐	☐	A great war called Armageddon will erupt in the Middle East (see Joel 3:14; Zechariah 12:11; Revelation 16:14–21)
☐	☐	☐	The righteous Saints who have died will be resurrected and be caught up to meet Christ (see Doctrine and Covenants 45:45)
☐	☐	☐	Christ's foot will touch down on the Mount of Olives and split it (see Zechariah 14:4–7; Doctrine and Covenants 45:48)
☐	☐	☐	The gospel will be preached to every nation (see Matthew 24:14; Doctrine and Covenants 133:37)
☐	☐	☐	The Jews will return to Jerusalem and receive their promised land (see Amos 9:14; Zechariah 2:4–12; 2 Nephi 9:2)
☐	☐	☐	Christ will suddenly come to His temple (see Malachi 3:1)
☐	☐	☐	Two prophets will minister in Jerusalem for more than three years, then be killed, lie dead in the streets for three days, and then be taken up into heaven (see Revelation 11:3–11)
☐	☐	☐	Elijah the prophet will appear to turn the hearts of the fathers to the children and the children to the fathers (see Malachi 4:5–6)

FULFILLED	IN PROCESS	NOT STARTED	
❑	❑	❑	Water will flow from under the temple at Jerusalem and heal the waters of the Dead Sea (see Ezekiel 47:1–12; Zechariah 14:8)
❑	❑	❑	Pools of living water will spring up in the barren deserts (see Doctrine and Covenants 133:29)
❑	❑	❑	A great latter-day meeting with Christ, Adam, and other saints will take place in the valley of Adam-ondi-Ahman (see Daniel 7:13–14; 2 Thessalonians 1:8; Doctrine and Covenants 27:5–14; 107:53–57; 116:1)
❑	❑	❑	The Lamanites will blossom as a rose (see Doctrine and Covenants 49:24–25; 2 Nephi 30:6)
❑	❑	❑	The lost ten tribes will return from the north countries (see Doctrine and Covenants 133:26–34)
❑	❑	❑	God will send angels to preach the gospel (see Revelation 14:6–7)
❑	❑	❑	People will say that Christ delays His coming (see Doctrine and Covenants 45:26)
❑	❑	❑	The city of Zion, the New Jerusalem, will be built upon the American continent (see Articles of Faith 1:10; Isaiah 4:5–6; Ether 13:8)
❑	❑	❑	A great sign will be given in heaven that all the earth shall see together (see Doctrine and Covenants 88:93)
❑	❑	❑	Christ will appear in power and glory to rule and reign over the earth (see Isaiah 63:1–4; Matthew 24:27; Doctrine and Covenants 45:44; 133:46–48)

Remember, the purposes of these signs aren't to scare us, they are to help us recognize the signs of and become more prepared for the Second Coming. As the Lord said, "If ye are prepared ye shall not fear" (Doctrine and Covenants 38:30). When the Lord told some of these signs of the Second Coming to His disciples in Jerusalem, they "were troubled. And I said unto them: Be not troubled, for, when all these things shall come to pass, *ye may know that the promises which have been made unto you shall be fulfilled*" (Doctrine and Covenants 45:34–35; emphasis added). Seeing these signs fulfilled should help us see that God is in control, that soon evil will be defeated, and that we will have the privilege of living in the Millennium with the Lord and our loved ones.

When Will the Second Coming Be?

Would you believe us if we answered, "Tomorrow!"? President Joseph Fielding Smith said:

> I was asked, not long ago, if I could tell when the Lord would come. I answered, Yes; and I answer, Yes, now. I know when he will come. He will come *tomorrow*. We have his word for it. Let me read it:
>
> ". . . For after today cometh the burning—this is speaking after the manner of the Lord—for verily I say, *tomorrow* all the proud and they that do wickedly shall be as stubble. . . ." [Doctrine and Covenants 64:24; emphasis added].
>
> So the Lord is coming, I say, *tomorrow*. Then let us be prepared. . . . We are living in the Saturday Evening of Time. [One day for the Lord is equal to a thousand years of our time. See Doctrine and Covenants 77:6–7.] This is the 6th day now drawing to its close. When the Lord says it is today until his coming, that, I think, is what he has in mind, for he shall come in the morning of the Sabbath, or seventh day of the earth's temporal existence, to inaugurate the millennial reign and to take his rightful place as King of kings and Lord of lords, to rule and reign upon the earth, as it is his right.[1]

If the Lord is coming "tomorrow" we definitely need to prepare "today."

But what if Jesus really *did* come tomorrow? What would you do?

Elder Dallin H. Oaks said:

> What if the day of His coming were tomorrow? If we knew that we would meet the Lord tomorrow—through our premature death or through His unexpected coming—what would we do today? What confessions would we make? What practices would we discontinue? What accounts would we settle? What forgivenesses would we extend? What testimonies would we bear?
>
> If we would do those things then, why not now?[2]

What Can I Do to Prepare for the Second Coming?

Let's look at three keys to preparing for the Second Coming:

1. Take the Holy Spirit as our guide.

2. Stand in holy places.

3. Look to the modern prophets to discern the signs and times of the Second Coming.

Take the Holy Spirit As Our Guide

Perhaps the best thing we can do to prepare for the Second Coming is to live so that we have the Holy Ghost with us in our daily life. We read in *True to the Faith*, "Do not concern yourself with the exact timing of the Savior's Second Coming. Instead, live so that you will be prepared whenever He comes."[3] We can know if we are prepared for the Second Coming if we have the Spirit of the Lord with us. The Lord gave us this key when He said of His Second Coming: "For they that are wise and have received the truth, and *have taken the Holy Spirit for their guide*, and have not been deceived—verily I say unto you, they shall not be hewn down and cast into the fire, but shall abide the day" (Doctrine and Covenants 45:57; emphasis added). As we live worthy of the Spirit, we will be guided, strengthened, and protected in the days leading up to the Second Coming.

Stand in Holy Places

Doctrine and Covenants 45 gives us another key to prepare for the Second Coming. The Lord said, "My disciples shall stand in holy places, and shall not be moved" (Doctrine and Covenants 45:32). Elder Dallin H. Oaks explained: "What are those 'holy places'? Surely they include the temple and its covenants faithfully kept. Surely they include a home where children are treasured and parents are respected. Surely the holy places include our posts of duty assigned by priesthood authority, including missions and callings faithfully fulfilled in branches, wards, and stakes."[4]

Clearly standing in holy places includes *not* standing in *unholy* places. By avoiding the evil that is all around us, we will have the Spirit in greater abundance. As we stand in holy places, our lives, homes, wards, and stakes will "be for a defense, and for a refuge from the storm" (Doctrine and Covenants 115:6). Stay active in the Church, and you will be actively ready for the Second Coming.

> Think about the places where you have "stood" (literally, or perhaps figuratively through the Internet or other media) in the past week. Were they holy places? Were there any holy places that you should have stood in but didn't? Based on your analysis, make a plan to stand only in holy places this next week.

Look to the Modern Prophets to Discern the Signs and Times of the Second Coming

The scriptures tell us that "the Lord will come as a thief in the night" (2 Peter 3:10). Many people will be caught totally by surprise and unprepared when Jesus comes again. Anyone who tells you that they can calculate or know the hour or day of the Second Coming is leading you astray. Joseph Smith taught, "Jesus Christ never did reveal to any man the precise time that He would come. Go and read the Scriptures, and you cannot find anything that specifies the exact hour He would come; and all that say so are false teachers."[5]

However, the scriptures also tell us that although "the hour and the day no man knoweth" (Doctrine and Covenants 49:7), the faithful will not be caught totally off guard. Listen to what the Lord said to the Saints: "The coming of the Lord draweth nigh, and it overtaketh the world as a thief in the night—therefore, gird up your loins, that you may be the children of light, and that day shall not overtake you as a thief" (Doctrine and Covenants 106:4–5; emphasis added).

The Apostle Paul gave an analogy of the Second Coming, likening it to a woman who is expecting to have a baby. She may not know the exact day she will deliver the child—and the day she goes into labor may be unexpected—but as she pays attention to the time and also the signs of her body, she can know for certain when the time is close (see 1 Thessalonians 5:3). Paul said, "But ye, brethren, are not in darkness, that that day [of the Second Coming] should overtake you as a thief. Ye are all the children of light, and the children of the day: we are not of the night, nor of darkness" (1 Thessalonians 5:4–5). As we become "children of light" by studying the scriptures and following the modern prophets, the Second Coming will not be a surprise to us.

We testify that the Lord will come again, and that it will be a glorious time for the faithful. Let us continue to prepare ourselves, and continue to "prepare the world for the Second Coming of the Savior."[6]

Still Have Questions?

What if Jesus returns as a child or in a different form than we are looking for?

Sometimes people say that Jesus will return as a child or in some other way. In Joseph Smith's day, a woman named Ann Lee claimed that she was Jesus and He had returned as a woman. The Lord told Joseph Smith in a revelation that "the Son of Man cometh not in the form of a woman, neither of a man traveling on the earth. Wherefore, be not deceived, but continue in steadfastness, looking forth for the [scriptural signs of the second coming]" (Doctrine and Covenants 49:22–23). We know what Jesus will look like when He returns, and His return won't be a secret to the world (see Doctrine and Covenants 88:93).

What if the Second Coming happens before I can have a family?

Some teenagers worry that they will never have the opportunity to have a family because the Second Coming will bring about the end of the world. President Boyd K. Packer said to the youth, "Sometimes you might be tempted to think as I did from time to time in my youth: 'The way things are going, the world's going to be over with. The end of the world is going to come before I get to where I should be.' Not so! You can look forward to doing it right—getting married, having a family, seeing your children and grandchildren, maybe even great-grandchildren."[7]

How does paying my tithing relate to the Second Coming?

While we might not think of tithing as being connected to the Second Coming, it is. In the Doctrine and Covenants we read, "Behold, now it is called today until the coming of the Son of Man, and verily it is a day of sacrifice, and a day for the tithing of my people; *for he that is tithed shall not be burned at his coming*" (Doctrine and Covenants 64:23; emphasis added). The Lord has promised that if we are faithful tithe payers, we will not be burned at the Second Coming.

Teach the Plan!

Christ's Return to Earth

Objective: To help us understand and prepare for the Second Coming of Jesus Christ.

Attention Getter: Teach the Plan #1. Show a painting of the Second Coming of Christ and ask your children if that is how they picture the event. Read Doctrine and Covenants 133:48, which suggests that the Lord will be wearing red when He returns.

Attention Getter: Experiment upon the Word: Test how many of these signs your children know by having them guess what they mean. Ask them if they know the signs of the Second Coming. Have them list as many signs of the Second Coming that they can think of in one minute.

Lesson Activity: Teach the Plan #3. Go to http://www.seek.deseretbook.com/big picture and download a copy of the signs of the Second Coming. Have your family divide into groups and discuss which signs have been fulfilled, are in process, or have yet to be started and why they think that. Have each group review the entire list. You might ask your children to discuss signs they know of that aren't included on this list.

Discussion Questions: The following questions may help your children in understanding, identifying, and applying some gospel truths related to Christ's Second Coming.

Teach the Plan #2. Why do you think the Second Coming will be a great day for some people, but terrible for others? How will it be great? How will it be terrible?

Teach the Plan #4. Read the quote by Elder Dallin H. Oaks. Then ask, "If Jesus' Second Coming were tomorrow, what would you do today?"

Teach the Plan #5. Ask, "Where are some of your personal 'holy places' where you are able to feel of and be influenced by God's Spirit? What might be the difference between 'standing' in holy places and merely 'visiting' holy places?"

Teach the Plan #6. Ask, "What have the modern prophets told us recently that you think might apply to our preparation for the Second Coming?"

Invitation to Act: Invite your children to do the Live the Plan activity and evaluate the places where they have stood in the past week. Follow up with them later to discuss the places where they were able to be influenced by God's Spirit and the places they might have labeled as "unholy" places.

13

A Thousand Years of Peace

Let's just get this straight right off the bat: The Millennium has nothing to do with the *Millennium Falcon* from *Star Wars*.

Yes, they share the same first name, and yes, there will be falcons in the Millennium, and yes, they both take place in the future, but one is real and the other is fake. (Sorry, Chewbacca.) So what is "the Millennium" and what does it have to do with us? Let's take a look at perhaps the most exciting thousand years to come.

What Is the Millennium?

 A millennium is a thousand years of time. When the scriptures and prophets talk about *the* Millennium, they are talking about the thousand years of peace and righteousness that will follow Christ's Second Coming. One thousand years! And we thought the Nephites had it good when they had their two hundred years of "no contention" (see 4 Nephi 1:1–26). The Millennium will be a time when the "whole earth is at rest" and we "break forth into singing" (2 Nephi 24:7) because Christ has returned, loved ones have been resurrected, evil and wickedness are gone, sin has ceased, sorrow is forgotten, and the earth is "full of the knowledge of the Lord, as the waters cover the sea" (Isaiah 11:9).

What Happens in the Millennium?

When Christ returns in glory and the Millennium begins, some really cool things are going to happen. Here are only a few:

Christ Will Reign Personally over the Earth

 During the Millennium, Jesus will "reign personally upon the earth" (Articles of Faith 1:10). Christ will assume His rightful role as king, and "Jesus will rule both the Church and the government. All laws will be based on true and righteous principles."[1] Joseph Smith said that "Christ and the resurrected Saints will reign over the earth during the thousand years. They will not probably dwell upon the earth, but will visit it when they please, or when it is necessary to govern it."[2]

Pop quiz! What are the capital cities of the following countries?

United States	Tokyo
Austria	Mexico City
Japan	Vienna
Mongolia	Ulaanbaatar
Italy	Santiago
Chile	Washington DC
Tonga	Rome
Kenya	Riyadh
Saudi Arabia	Nairobi
Mexico	Nuku'alofa

During the Millennium, "There will be two capital cities. One will be in Jerusalem. The other capital will be the New Jerusalem, in the United States."[3] The scriptures teach us that the capital city of the New Jerusalem will be on "the American continent" (Articles of Faith 1:10) in the state of Missouri (see Doctrine and Covenants 84:2–4).

(Answers: United States: Washington, D.C.; Austria: Vienna; Japan: Tokyo; Mongolia: Ulaanbaatar; Italy: Rome; Chile: Santiago; Tonga: Nuku'alofa; Kenya: Nairobi; Saudi Arabia: Riyadh; Mexico: Mexico City.)

Satan Will Be Bound

One of the reasons why the Millennium will be so great is because "During the Millennium, Satan will be bound. This means he will not have power to tempt those who are living at that time."[4] Doctrine and Covenants 101:28 says, "And in that day [the Millennium] Satan shall not have power to tempt any man." Some people have mistakenly taught that the reason for this will simply be because people will be so righteous during the Millennium that Satan won't have any power over them as he tries to tempt them. That is not true.

Joseph Fielding Smith taught, "There are many among us who teach that the binding of Satan will be merely the binding which those dwelling on the earth will place upon him by their refusal to hear his enticings. This is not so. He will not have the privilege during that period of time to tempt any man."[5]

> **LIVE THE PLAN** President Spencer W. Kimball taught: "When Satan is bound in a single home—when Satan is bound in a single life—the Millennium has already begun in that home, in that life."[6] We invite you to consider ways you can inch one step closer to your personal millennium by acting more Christlike at home.

There Will Be Peace on Earth

One of the signs of the Second Coming is that there will be "wars and rumors of wars" (Doctrine and Covenants 45:26). When Jesus returns and all during the entire thousand years of the Millennium, *there will be no war!* Period.

As a matter of fact, there will be no contention and no enmity between anyone, because contention is of the devil (see 3 Nephi 11:29) and Satan will be bound. Isaiah teaches that during the Millennium even animals will stop fighting and "the wolf also shall dwell with the lamb" (Isaiah 11:6). "Nation shall not lift up sword against nation, neither shall they learn war any more" (Isaiah 2:4; see also Doctrine and Covenants 101:26). That means no more fighting with parents, friends, or even annoying siblings. Everyone will get along peacefully. Hallelujah!

The Dead Will Be Resurrected

When Jesus comes again, all the righteous Saints who have died and not been resurrected but who are worthy to go to the celestial kingdom will be resurrected and caught up to meet Christ. "And they who have slept in their graves shall come forth, for their graves shall be opened" (Doctrine and Covenants 88:97). At some point in the Millennium, the dead who are worthy of the terrestrial kingdom will be resurrected. And at some point at the end of the thousand years of the Millennium, those who are to receive the lowest kingdom—the telestial—will be resurrected (see Doctrine and Covenants 88:97–101). (For more on resurrection, see chapter 16.)

There Will Be No Sickness and No Death

During the Millennium, nobody will die and be buried. Nobody will even get sick because during those thousand years "there will be no disease."[7] No one will die prematurely, but everyone will live "until he is old" (Doctrine and Covenants 101:30). When they do die, "they shall not sleep in the dust, but they shall be changed [resurrected] in the twinkling of an eye" (Doctrine and Covenants 63:51). Can you imagine that! No more funerals. Instead maybe we will have "twinkled" celebrations!

The Earth Will Be Renewed

Have you ever thought it would be cool to live in a place like the Garden of Eden? Well, during the Millennium, you'll get the chance to. The Prophet Joseph Smith taught that during the Millennium, "the earth will be renewed and receive its paradisiacal glory" (Articles of Faith 1:10). Currently our earth is in a telestial condition, and when the Millennium is ushered in the earth will be upgraded to a terrestrial state.

Elder Bruce R. McConkie wrote, "Thus, the earth is to go back to the primeval, paradisiacal, or terrestrial state that prevailed in the days of the Garden of Eden. . . . It will then be a new heaven and a new earth, and again health, peace, and joy will prevail upon its face (D&C 101:23–32; Isa. 65:17–25; Mal. 3:1–6; 4:1–6; *Man: His Origin and Destiny,* pp. 380–397.)"[8]

So the earth will go through some major changes—from a telestial state, to a terrestrial, to a celestial. The *Encyclopedia of Mormonism* teaches, "Because of the Fall of Adam and Eve, [the earth] was transformed to a telestial state, or the present mortal earth. This interval will end with the return of the Savior, after which the earth will be changed to a terrestrial state and prepared during the Millennium for its final transformation into a celestial sphere after the Millennium (D&C 88:18–19)."[9]

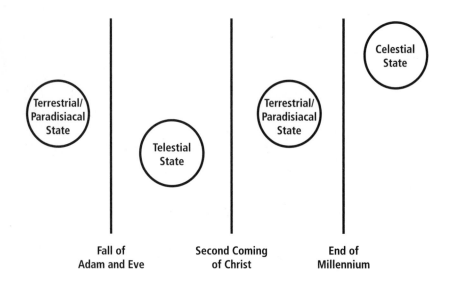

God Will Reveal All Things

During the Millennium, the Lord will "reveal all things— things which have passed, and hidden things which no man knew, things of the earth, by which it was made, and the purpose and the end thereof—things most precious, things that are above, and things that are beneath, things that are in the earth, and upon the earth, and in heaven" (Doctrine and Covenants 101:32–34). Isaiah says that in the Millennium our answers to questions will come so fast that "before they call, I will answer; and while they are yet speaking, I will hear" (Isaiah 65:24).

What Will I Do in the Millennium?

We know some teenagers who don't want the Second Coming to happen and the Millennium to start because they don't want the world to end. They still want to have a life, date, go on missions, go to school, get married, have kids, and have a job. The good news is, you'll still get to do all that.

The better news is, you'll get to do all of that without any temptation, boredom, sickness, dating drama, contention, or rebellious children of your own. *Gospel Principles* teaches, "In many ways, life will be much as it is now, except that everything will be done in righteousness."[10] And Elder Bruce R. McConkie taught, "During the millennial era, . . . mortality as such will continue. Children will be born, grow up, marry, advance to old age, and pass through the equivalent of death. Crops will be planted, harvested, and eaten; industries will be expanded, cities built, and education fostered; men will continue to care for their own needs, handle their own affairs, and enjoy the full endowment of free agency."[11]

Marriage, Children, Homes, and Jobs

We know from the scriptures that in the Millennium we will still live in houses, work, and have jobs. Isaiah says of our millennial work, "And they shall build houses, and inhabit them; and they shall plant vineyards, and eat the fruit of them" (Isaiah 65:21). We also know that righteous dating, courtship, love, and marriage will continue in the Millennium. The scriptures teach us that couples "shall multiply and wax strong, and their children shall grow up without sin unto salvation" (Doctrine and Covenants 45:58).

How cool will it be to be a parent in the Millennium? No whining, no fighting, no rebellion, no attitude—not that you give any of that to your parents now, right? All of your kids will grow up righteous, live until they are old, be resurrected in the twinkling of an eye, and inherit the celestial kingdom.

Elder Bruce R. McConkie said, "Billions of spirits will come to earth during the Millennium, when Satan is bound, when there is peace on earth, when there is no sorrow because there is no death, when they will not be confronted with the evil and carnality that face us. They will grow up without sin unto salvation."[12]

Missionary Work

Much of our work in the Millennium will be centered on missionary work. Although Christ will have returned, the wicked will have been destroyed, and Satan will be bound, people will still need to be taught the gospel.

True to the Faith teaches, "During the Millennium, all people on the earth will be good and just, but many will not have received the fulness of the gospel. Consequently, members of the Church will participate in missionary work."[13]

Joseph Fielding Smith taught, "There will be millions of people, Catholics, Protestants, agnostics, Mohammedans, people of all classes, and all beliefs, still permitted to remain upon the face of the earth, but they will be those who have lived clean lives, those who have been free from wickedness and corruption. All who belong, by virtue of their good lives, to [at least] the terrestrial order . . . will remain upon the face of the earth during the millennium."[14]

"People will still have their agency, and for a time many will be free to continue with their religions and ideas. Eventually everyone will confess that Jesus Christ is the Savior."[15] Isaiah says that missionary work will spread across the world in the Millennium until eventually "the earth shall be full of the knowledge of the Lord, as the waters cover the sea" (Isaiah 11:9).

Those who are not members of the Church who live during the Millennium will still "be those who have lived virtuous and honest lives. These people will inherit either the terrestrial or celestial kingdom."[16]

Temple Work

Another great work we will do in the Millennium is temple work: "Members of the Church will also participate in temple work during the Millennium. The Saints will continue to build temples and receive ordinances in behalf of their kindred dead. Guided by revelation, they will prepare records of their ancestors all the way back to Adam and Eve."[17]

Brigham Young taught that in the Millennium "we will have revelations to know our forefathers clear back to Father Adam and Mother Eve, and we will enter into the temples of God and officiate for them. Then man will be sealed to man until the chain is made perfect back to Adam, so that there will be a perfect chain of priesthood from Adam to the winding-up scene. This will be the work of the Latter-day Saints in the millennium."[18]

What Happens at the End of the Millennium?

Unfortunately, there will be a short period of time after the thousand years of the Millennium when Satan will be loosed, wickedness will begin again, people will turn away from God, and peace will be taken from the earth. We do not know how long this period of time will be. The scriptures only say "that when the thousand years are ended, and men again begin to deny their God, then will I spare the earth but for a little season" (Doctrine and Covenants 29:22).

After Satan is loosed for this little season at the end of the Millennium, preparations will happen for a great war between the righteous and the wicked, and then Satan and his followers will be cast off forever. The scriptures teach,

> And then [Satan] shall be loosed for a little season, that he may gather together his armies.
> And Michael [Adam], the seventh angel, even the archangel, shall gather together his armies, even the hosts of heaven.
> And the devil shall gather together his armies; even the hosts of hell, and shall come up to battle against Michael and his armies.
> And then cometh the battle of the great God; and the devil and his armies shall be cast away into their own place, that they shall not have power over the saints any more at all. (Doctrine and Covenants 88:111–14)

Following this great last battle and the destruction of the wicked, Satan will be cast out forever, and the earth "will be changed into a celestial kingdom"[19] and become like a "sea of glass" (Doctrine and Covenants 130:7), and attain "its sanctified, immortal, and eternal state" (Doctrine and Covenants 77:1–2). Then "the meek of the earth shall inherit it" (Doctrine and Covenants 88:17) and it will become the celestial kingdom, where "it shall be crowned with glory, even with the presence of God the Father; that bodies who are of the celestial kingdom may possess it forever and ever" (Doctrine and Covenants 88:19–20).

Teach the Plan!

A Thousand Years of Peace

Objective: To help learners understand and look forward to the millennial reign of Jesus Christ.

Attention Getter: Teach the Plan #1: Ask your children if they've ever heard of a ship called "The Thousand Year Falcon." Then show them a picture of the *Millennium Falcon* from *Star Wars* and ask them to tell you why you called it "The Thousand Year Falcon." Read the paragraph on what the Millennium really is.

Attention Getter: Experiment upon the Word: Take the capital city pop quiz and then ask your kids if they can name the two Millennial capital cities. Have one of your children read the paragraph explaining where those two capital cities will be.

Lesson Activity: Teach the Plan #2: Give each member of your family a blank piece of paper and a pen and have them list as many things as they can think of about what will happen in the Millennium. The person who has the most things mentioned in the chapter wins.

Discussion Questions: The following questions may help your children in understanding, identifying, and applying some gospel truths related to the Millennium:

Teach the Plan #3: Ask, "How do you think things will be different when Jesus is both the leader of the Church and the leader of the world governments?"

Teach the Plan #4: Ask, "If all things will be revealed in the Millennium, what are the top two or three questions you would like to have answered?"

Teach the Plan #5: Have your children discuss how they think the Millennium will—and won't—change what they want to do with their lives.

Invitation to Act: Read the quote from President Spencer W. Kimball next to the Live the Plan icon. Have your family discuss different ways you can implement this idea—that the Millennium can start today in our personal lives—in your home. Invite your family members to act on what they feel prompted to do.

Act III

Life after Death

14

What Happens When We Die?

 The US Census Bureau estimates that more than 150,000 people die *every day* across the world.[1] A hundred people somewhere in the world die every minute. What happened to those 150,000 people who died today? Where did their spirits go? Are they near us? Are they still themselves? Can they think and act and move? Or are they gone forever?

Questions about death and what happens to us after we die are among some of the most intriguing and often asked questions by people around the world. Many other faiths have their ideas about what happens to us after we die. Some religions teach that the spirit ceases to exist, while others teach that we are reincarnated (come back to earth as different people), and still others teach that the spirit goes straight to heaven or hell.

There are even people who write and talk about "near-death experiences"—people who momentarily died and then came back to life—who try to explain what they saw and what happens to us after we die. While we don't discount those experiences, we also don't rely on them for information about the next life. The scriptures and prophets have already explained what happens to us after we die.

What Happens to Us When We Die?

Death is the separation of the spirit from the mortal body. We know that our *spirits* are eternal and cannot die (see Mosiah 2:28; Doctrine and Covenants 93:33). Born of our

A Comparison of World Religions[2]

	Buddhism	Reincarnation (understood differently than in Hinduism, with no surviving soul) until enlightenment is gained
	Catholicism	Temporary purgatory to pay for sins, then go to heaven or hell
	Hare Krishna	Reincarnation until united with the Godhead
	Hinduism	Reincarnation until enlightenment is gained
	Islam (Muslim)	Go to paradise or to hell
	Jehovah's Witness	Heaven for 144,000 chosen Witnesses, eternity on new earth for other Witnesses. All others annihilated. No hell.
	Judaism	Not historically emphasized. Beliefs vary from no afterlife to shadowy existence in the world to come (similar to heaven).
	Seventh-day Adventist	A "peaceful pause" after death until the coming of Christ, then resurrection to judgment, followed by eternity in heaven or nonexistence. No hell.
	Sikhism	Reincarnation until karma is resolved, then merge with God
	Taoism	Revert back to state of nonbeing, which is simply the other side of being

heavenly parents in the premortal existence, our eternal spirits entered our physical body here on earth. After the physical body dies, our spirit becomes separated from our body and continues to live. When our spirit leaves our body, we enter the spirit world. The spirit world is divided into two places: spirit paradise and spirit prison.

Those who go to spirit paradise are those who have been righteous and obedient to the commandments of God. They "are received into a state of happiness, which is called paradise, a state of rest, a state of peace, where they shall rest from all their troubles and from all care, and sorrow" (Alma 40:12; see also Doctrine and Covenants 138:22). In spirit paradise, the righteous are free from the temptations of the adversary. President George Q. Cannon taught that "when death comes, Satan's power ceases [over the righteous souls in spirit paradise]. He can no more afflict or torment or tempt or annoy those who are thus faithful. His power over them ceases forever. . . . He can do nothing to interfere with their happiness."[3]

Those who go to spirit prison are "those who [have] died in their sins, without a knowledge of the truth, or in transgression, having rejected the prophets" (Doctrine and Covenants 138:32). Those who are in spirit prison can still be influenced by the adversary, and can use their agency to rebel and sin or to obey and be righteous (see Alma 40:13–14). "These spirits [in prison] have agency and may be enticed by both good and evil."[4]

Although righteous missionaries are sent from spirit paradise to teach those in spirit prison, there is a great "gulf," or separation, so that those in spirit prison cannot freely pass into spirit paradise, except on conditions of repentance (see 1 Nephi 15:28–30; Luke 16:26; *Gospel Principles*, 243–44). In *True to the Faith*, we read, "The spirits in prison are 'taught faith in God, repentance from sin, vicarious baptism for the remission of sins, the gift of the Holy Ghost by the laying on of hands, and all other principles of the gospel that [are] necessary for them to know' (D&C 138:33–34). If they accept the principles of the gospel, repent of their sins, and accept ordinances performed in their behalf in temples, they will be welcomed into paradise."[5]

What Does the Spirit World Look like, and Where Is It Located?

President Ezra Taft Benson said of the spirit world: "Sometimes the veil between this life and the life beyond becomes very thin. Our loved ones who have passed on are not far from us."[6]

So where are they? Well, the spirit world is a lot like this earth—because it is on this earth. Yep, that's right. When we die we don't travel to some unknown universe. Our spirits stay right here on earth. Brigham Young asked, "Where is the spirit world? *It is right here.* Do the good and evil spirits go together? Yes, they do. Do they both inhabit one kingdom? Yes, they do. Do they go to the sun? No. Do they go beyond the boundaries of the organized earth? No, they do not. They are brought forth upon this earth, for the express purpose of inhabiting it to all eternity. Where else are you going? Nowhere else, only as you may be permitted."[7]

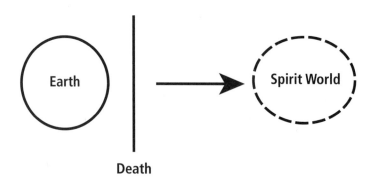

We commonly see the spirit world drawn as a separate world from this earth, as though we are going somewhere else when we die. Although the spirit world is in a different spiritual dimension, a more accurate drawing would be something like this:

We do not leave this earth when we go to the spirit world.

What Will I Be like in the Spirit World?

Perhaps the most important thing to know about what we will be like in the spirit world is that we won't be much different than we are here on earth. The prophet Alma taught us that the "same spirit which doth possess your bodies at the time that ye go out of this life, that same spirit will have power to possess your body in that eternal world" (Alma 34:34). In other words, we will still be ourselves in the spirit world—if we love the Lord here, we will love him there; if we don't like church here, we probably won't magically like it there.

We read in *Gospel Principles* that people in the spirit world "carry with them from earth their attitudes of devotion or antagonism toward things of righteousness (see Alma 34:34). They have the same appetites and desires that they had when they lived on earth."[8] There will be one major difference though: we won't feel the effects of a mortal body. Headaches? Gone. Bad knee? History. Bad hair day? We're not sure ☺.

Brigham Young taught that in the spirit world, "My spirit is set free, I thirst no more, I want to sleep no more, I hunger no more, I tire no more, I run, I walk, I labor, I go, I come, I do this, I do that, whatever is required of me, nothing like pain or weariness, I am full of life, full of vigor, and I enjoy the presence of my heavenly Father, by the power of his Spirit."[9]

And speaking of hair and knees, what will we look like physically in the spirit world? Will we be floating masses of spirit? Heavens, no.

We will look just like we do here, in the same form and body—with legs and arms and all of the above. When the brother of Jared saw Jesus, he saw His spirit body. Jesus taught him, "Behold, this body, which ye now behold, is the body of my spirit; and man have I created after the body of my spirit; and even as I appear unto thee to be in the spirit will I appear unto my people in the flesh" (Ether 3:16).

In *Gospel Fundamentals,* we read, "In the spirit world our spirits will have the same form as when we lived on the earth with a body of flesh and bones. We will look as we do here."[10] Additionally, all spirits will be in adult form in the spirit world. People "were adults before their mortal existence, and they are in adult form after death, even if they die as infants or children."[11]

The scriptures teach us, "There is no such thing as immaterial matter. All spirit is matter, but it is more fine or pure, and can only be discerned by purer eyes; we cannot see it; but when our bodies are purified we shall see that it is all matter" (Doctrine and Covenants 131:7–8). When we see our loved ones in the spirit world who have passed on before us, we will be able to embrace and hold and touch them spirit to spirit.

Elder Charles W. Penrose taught, "Spirit is a substance, it is not immaterial; it may have some properties that are different from that which we see and handle, which we call matter, but it is a reality, a substantial reality. And spirit can understand spirit and grasp spirit. A spiritual person can take the hand of another spiritual person and it is substantial. . . . A spiritual substance, organized into form, oc-cupies room and space just as much in its sphere as these natural particles occupy in this sphere."[12]

What Will I Do in the Spirit World?

When we die and enter the spirit world, we will be there un-til the day of our resurrection. *Gospel Principles* teaches, "The spirit world is a place of waiting, working, learning, and, for the righteous, resting from care and sorrow. Our spirits will live there until we are ready for our resurrection. Then our mortal bodies will once more unite with our spirits, and we will receive the degree of glory we have prepared for."[13]

Obviously, what we will do in the spirit world depends a lot on what type of person we are during our mortal life. Many people in spirit paradise will be building up the kingdom of God by preaching the gospel to the spirits in prison (see Doctrine and Covenants 138:33–34, 57).

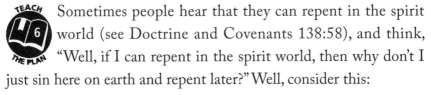 Sometimes people hear that they can repent in the spirit world (see Doctrine and Covenants 138:58), and think, "Well, if I can repent in the spirit world, then why don't I just sin here on earth and repent later?" Well, consider this:

- Try improving your guitar skills without a guitar. Go ahead. Try it!
- Try improving your texting skills without a keyboard. Seriously, do it!
- Try improving your free throw shot without holding a basketball. Can you?

What do those exercises have to do with repenting in the spirit world? Well, in order to improve our spirit, it's really useful to have a body. Without it, it's a lot harder to improve—just like it's a lot harder to improve our music skills without a musical instrument.

Without a body, it becomes much more difficult to repent and change our character. Perhaps that is one reason why our spirits will look forward to being back in our bodies (see Doctrine and Covenants 138:50). Elder Hartman Rector Jr. said,

> Yes, it is possible to repent in the spirit world, although we are given to understand that it is much more difficult to repent there because we will not have our physical bodies to help us. . . .

President Brigham Young said it is a hundred times easier to repent here on the earth than it is in the spirit world. . . . Now is the best time to repent.[14]

So, just like how becoming a better basketball player is best done with an actual basketball, "repentance is best achieved while one still has a body."[15]

EXPERIMENT Gather a few items that are small enough to fit in a UPON THE WORD glass jar—and that you don't mind getting wet. The items should represent different material or tangible things in this world (for example, a toy car could represent a real car, a lipstick tube could represent physical beauty, and a penny could represent material wealth). Fill the jar halfway to the brim with clean water. Then place the small items you have gathered in the water.

Add a few drops of food coloring to the water as well. Swirl the jar so the color spreads throughout the water. Place a strainer on top of a second, empty jar and pour the colored water and the worldly items through the strainer. Obviously, only the colored water makes it into the next jar.

What lessons from this do you see in your life? What can you do to apply them?

The truth is, we will only take those things with us into the spirit world which are intangible. We will take things such as our knowledge, our testimony, and our character. We will take memories, attitudes, and personalities. We will take faith, hope, and charity. We will take eternal covenants, temple ordinances, and priesthood offices with us. In other words, we will take all those things with us that money cannot buy and the world cannot offer. We can only take what is eternal. If that is all we take with us, then isn't that what we should focus on the most?

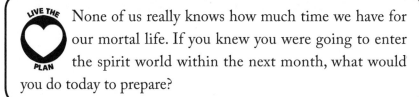 None of us really knows how much time we have for our mortal life. If you knew you were going to enter the spirit world within the next month, what would you do today to prepare?

Still Have Questions?

What do baptisms for the dead have to do with the spirit world?

Everybody has the chance to hear and accept the gospel— whether in this life or in the spirit world. Since God requires that all men be baptized to be saved (see Mark 16:16; John 3:5), it is logical He will make it possible for all people to be baptized if they want to. *True to the Faith* teaches, "People who have died without essential gospel ordinances may receive those ordinances through the work done in temples."[16] The doctrine of temple work for the dead—including performing baptisms for the dead—is the only logical answer to the question of how God can require all people to be baptized and still be a just, fair God.

Do we believe in reincarnation?

Reincarnation is defined as the "rebirth of the soul in another body."[17] Although we respect others' ideas about death and the next life, we know from the doctrines of the restored gospel that the spirits of all people go to the spirit world after this life, and that all will be resurrected (see Alma 40:11; 11:42–43).

Teach the Plan!

What Happens When We Die?

Objective: To help learners more clearly understand what happens after we die and what we will be like in the spirit world so we can better prepare for the time when we will die and enter the spirit world.

Attention Getter: Ask your children how many people they think die every day across the world. After everyone has made a guess, read the text next to Teach the Plan #1 and discuss with your family where all those thousands of people who die each day go.

Attention Getter: Ask your children if they would like to know what they will be like in the spirit world after they die. Have them close their eyes, then open them. Say, "Congratulations, this is what you are like in the spirit world." Read the material next to Teach the Plan #4 about what we will be like in the spirit world and discuss how that knowledge might influence our behavior here on earth. Use this activity to lead into a discussion about what the spirit world is and what we will do there.

Lesson Activity: Do the Experiment upon the Word activity and fill a jar with small items that represent worldly possessions or ideas. Have one of your children put the items in the jar and have him or her tell you what each of those items might represent. Have another child pour the water in and mix in the food coloring. Have him or her discuss what the drops could symbolize. Then strain the objects out and discuss with your family what lessons they learned about this life, and the next, from this object lesson.

Lesson Activity: Teach the Plan #6: Some people wonder why we should worry about being obedient now if we can repent in the spirit world. Have your kids attempt the guitar playing, texting exercise, and basketball shot as described. Read the quote from Elder Hartman Rector Jr. and discuss with your family why, even if we can continue to repent and improve in the spirit world, it is best to repent while we still have a mortal body.

Discussion Questions: The following questions may help your children in understanding, identifying, and applying some gospel truths related to life after death.

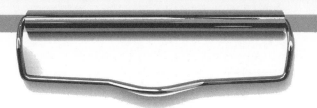

Teach the Plan #2: Ask, "What do you think happens when we die? Why do you think death is part of God's plan?"

Teach the Plan #3: Ask, "How does knowing that the spirit world is here on earth change or influence your perspectives of death and those who have died?"

Teach the Plan #5: Ask, "How does it change your perspective of the spirit world to know that in the spirit world our spirit bodies are bodies of spiritual substance and matter?"

Invitation to Act: Ask the question next to the Live the Plan icon. Invite your family to act on the promptings that come to their mind and heart as they consider that question.

15

Who Will Go to the Celestial Kingdom?

TEACH 4 1 THE PLAN Please start this chapter by taking this poll:

> If you died and were judged today, which eternal kingdom do you think you would go to?
>
> A. Celestial (the top)
> B. Terrestrial (the middle)
> C. Telestial (the bottom)

If you picked the terrestrial kingdom, you're not alone. Take a look at these numbers from 184 ninth-grade seminary students in Salt Lake City, Utah, who took this same poll:

> 30%–Celestial kingdom
> 54%–Terrestrial kingdom
> 16%–Telestial kingdom

A group of Especially for Youth (EFY) participants were also asked to take this same poll. We broke down their answers by age group. Take a look at the diagram on the following page.

Notice what happens as teens in this sample get older? The fourteen-year-olds were about an even split between who thinks they will go to the celestial and terrestrial kingdoms. Turning fifteen apparently brings a magical boost of celestial confidence—almost 70

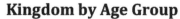

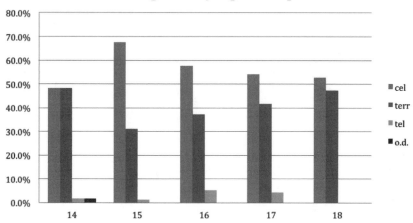

Kingdom by Age Group

percent of the fifteen-year-olds sampled thought they would make it to the celestial kingdom!

But then, as time goes on and people get older—perhaps as they make more frequent or serious mistakes—fewer and fewer of the teenagers surveyed thought they would go to the celestial kingdom, and more and more of them thought they would go to the terrestrial kingdom.

What about Heaven and Hell?

Before we discuss eternal kingdoms, let's get one thing clear: Latter-day Saints don't believe in heaven and hell the way other religions teach the concepts. We believe in three kingdoms of *heaven.* Three places of *glory.* Yes, there is spirit paradise and spirit prison (see chapter 14), which could be considered a heaven and a hell. But those are only temporary places where we go while we wait for the resurrection (see chapter 16). The Book of Mormon prophet Alma taught that people will only be in the spirit world "until the time of their resurrection" (Alma 40:14), at which time all people (except the sons of perdition) will be judged and go to one of the three degrees of heaven.

As Joseph Smith pondered on the truth that all of God's children would be resurrected, the Lord revealed the doctrine of three kingdoms and degrees of resurrected glory. The amazing thing is that although this doctrine of three degrees of glory seemed new and revolutionary to the majority of the Christian world when Joseph taught it, it is plainly taught in the New Testament. Paul talks about being "caught up to the third heaven" (2 Corinthians 12:2) in a vision, and he also tells us that there are "celestial bodies, and bodies terrestrial," and bodies telestial in the resurrection (1 Corinthians 15:40). Even Jesus tells us that "in my Father's house are many mansions" (John 14:2).

Elder Quentin L. Cook of the Quorum of the Twelve Apostles summarized it this way: "Because of the Atonement of Jesus Christ, all spirits blessed by birth [excepting sons of perdition] will ultimately be resurrected . . . and inherit kingdoms of glory that are superior to our existence here on earth."[1] Truly the Lord "saves all the works of his hands" (Doctrine and Covenants 76:43).

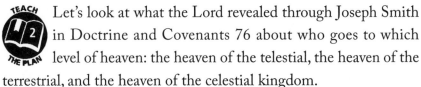 Let's look at what the Lord revealed through Joseph Smith in Doctrine and Covenants 76 about who goes to which level of heaven: the heaven of the telestial, the heaven of the terrestrial, and the heaven of the celestial kingdom.

What Is the Telestial Kingdom like, and Who Goes There?

The telestial kingdom is the lowest of the three kingdoms of heaven. While the celestial kingdom is compared to the glory of the sun, the terrestrial is compared to the glory of the moon, and the telestial kingdom is compared to the glory of the stars (see 1 Corinthians 15:40–42; Doctrine and Covenants 76:96–98). Even so, the telestial kingdom is still an amazingly beautiful and glorious place. As a matter of fact, the telestial kingdom is so glorious that when Joseph Smith saw it in a vision he said its glory "surpasses all understanding" (Doctrine and Covenants 76:89).

However, the telestial kingdom is nothing compared to the glory of the terrestrial kingdom, which is nothing compared to the glory of the celestial kingdom (see Doctrine and Covenants 76:89–92). And unfortunately, those who inherit the telestial kingdom will not live with God the Father or Jesus Christ.

So who goes to the telestial kingdom? They are those who "wilfully rebel against God" (3 Nephi 6:18) and desire to sin. Telestial people are those who never accept Jesus as the Christ nor follow His gospel in this world or in the spirit world (see Doctrine and Covenants 76:82, 101). They are people who on earth "were liars, thieves, murderers, false prophets, adulterers, and those who ridiculed sacred things."[2] People who go to the telestial kingdom will not be resurrected "until the last resurrection," at the end of the Millennium (Doctrine and Covenants 76:85). That's a long wait.

What Is the Terrestrial Kingdom like, and Who Goes There?

About half the youth surveyed believed they would go to the terrestrial kingdom. It's true, many members of the Church will go to the terrestrial kingdom, but not because they are imperfect or have made some mistakes. No, those who go to the terrestrial kingdom are those who rejected the chance to follow Jesus but still chose to live decent and good lives on earth. They are "honorable" people (Doctrine and Covenants 76:75) who weren't "valiant in the testimony of Jesus" (Doctrine and Covenants 76:79). This includes members and nonmembers of the Church. President Joseph Fielding Smith said, "Into the terrestrial will go all those who are honorable, who have been morally clean, *but who would not receive the gospel.*"[3]

Terrestrial people had the chance to follow Christ on earth and receive His gospel, but, for whatever reason, they didn't. Perhaps they were baptized into the gospel, but led wishy-washy lives. Although they are good people, terrestrial people are those who became distracted by the things of the world and "blinded by the craftiness of men" (Doctrine and Covenants 76:75). They are those "who received not the testimony of Jesus in the flesh, but afterwards received it" (Doctrine and Covenants 76:74), meaning that they had the chance to follow Christ here on earth—and rejected it—but then later decided to repent in the spirit world and follow Him.

The terrestrial kingdom "excels in all things the glory of the telestial, even in glory, and in power, and in might, and in dominion" (Doctrine and Covenants 76:91), but it is not as good as the celestial kingdom (see Doctrine and Covenants 76:92). The terrestrial kingdom will be visited by Jesus, but not by God the Father (see Doctrine and Covenants 76:77).

What Is the Celestial Kingdom like, and Who Goes There?

The revelation that tells us all about the three degrees of heaven—Doctrine and Covenants 76—is 119 verses long. However, only

- 12 verses are spent on the terrestrial kingdom,
- 16 verses are spent on the sons of perdition,
- 18 verses are spent on the telestial kingdom, but
- 26 verses are spent on the celestial kingdom!

Maybe we dwell more on the terrestrial kingdom than the Lord does. Clearly the Lord wants us to know about and focus on the celestial kingdom, so let's center our efforts on getting there!

To go to the celestial kingdom we need to be perfected—clean, holy, innocent, without spot—because "no unclean thing can inherit the kingdom of heaven" (Alma 11:37). You might be thinking, "That's impossible! No wonder nobody will go to the celestial kingdom!" And you're right—if it were up to us to be perfect and clean and holy on our own, none of us would make it.

No matter how many good works we do—no matter how many cookies we take to neighbors, no matter how many thousands of tables and chairs we set up, no matter how many times we go to church or attend the temple, and even if we paid 15 percent tithing, we could still not qualify ourselves to go to heaven on our own. King Benjamin said, "If ye should serve [God] with all your whole souls yet ye would be unprofitable servants" (Mosiah 2:21).

God commands us to be perfect (see Matthew 5:48; 3 Nephi 12:48), but we need to understand that we don't need to be perfect to go to heaven, we need to be *perfected.* Elder Russell M. Nelson taught that the commandment to be perfect "can come in full only after the Resurrection and only through the Lord."[4] We need to "come unto Christ, and be perfected in him" (Moroni 10:32). Perfection requires Jesus. It isn't something *we* do; it is something that is *done to us* by the Savior.

Although we can't qualify ourselves for salvation through our own works, we *can* qualify ourselves for Christ, and Christ can qualify us for the celestial kingdom. (See chapter 9.) If we will make and keep covenants with Christ, then Christ will perfect us. That is why Doctrine and Covenants 76 does *not* say anything about *us* needing to be perfect to go to heaven. It says that those who go to the celestial kingdom are those who

- "received the testimony of Jesus" (Doctrine and Covenants 76:51)
- "believed on his name" (Doctrine and Covenants 76:51)
- "were baptized" (Doctrine and Covenants 76:51)
- "receive the Holy Spirit" (Doctrine and Covenants 76:52)
- "overcome by faith" (Doctrine and Covenants 76:53)

If you meet these qualifications right now—and we're betting you do—then you are already on the celestial track!

Those who are exalted in the celestial kingdom will be "given all things" (Doctrine and Covenants 76:55), they will become "priests and kings" and receive of God's "fulness, and of his glory" (Doctrine and Covenants 76:56), "they are gods" (Doctrine and Covenants 76:58), and "all things are theirs" (Doctrine and Covenants 76:59), and they "shall dwell in the presence of God and his Christ forever and ever" (Doctrine and Covenants 76:62). Going to the celestial kingdom is our goal—and through Christ it is possible for all of us.

EXPERIMENT UPON THE WORD Find the nearest basketball hoop (perhaps an outside hoop, or a small rim that hangs over a door; if you don't have access to either one of those options, simply use an empty garbage can). Stand back about ten feet and try to make ten shots in a row. Most likely, you won't be able to, because—unless you're like Michael Jordan—most people aren't perfect shooters. What do you need when you miss a shot? A rebounder for the ball! Ask someone to be your rebounder so that, when you miss a shot, that person can rebound your missed shot and put the ball in the hoop.

What might this experience teach us about Christ, the Atonement, grace, and perfection? Discuss the analogy as a family.

Gospel Math 101%

TEACH THE PLAN 5 There are those who say if they just work hard enough, they can get themselves into heaven. If they just gain enough knowledge, if they just have the right attitude, then they can achieve the 101% standard of perfection and make it into heaven. But consider this (slightly humorous) mathematical exercise:

If

A B C D E F G H I J K L M N O P Q R S T U V W X Y Z

Is represented as

1 2 3 4 5 6 7 8 9 10 11 12 13 14 15 16 17 18 19 20 21 22 23 24 25 26

Then

H-A-R-D-W-O-R-K

8+1+18+4+23+15+18+11=98%

And

K-N-O-W-L-E-D-G-E

11+14+15+23+12+5+4+7+5=96%

But

A-T-T-I-T-U-D-E

1+20+20+9+20+21+4+5=100%

And look how far the love of God will take you:

L-O-V-E-O-F-G-O-D

12+15+22+5+15+6+7+15+4=101%

Therefore, while hard work and knowledge will get you close, and attitude will get you there, it's the love of God that will put you over the top!

What Will Life Be like in the Celestial Kingdom?

Elder Orson Pratt, one of the original twelve Apostles in this dispensation, gave one possible description of what the celestial kingdom might be like, saying,

> Heaven . . . [has] lands, houses, cities, vegetation, rivers, and animals; with thrones, temples, palaces, kings, princes, priests, and angels; with food, raiment, musical instruments, &c.; all of which are material. Indeed, the Saints' heaven is a redeemed, glorified, celestial, material creation, inhabited by glorified material beings, male and female, organized into families, embracing all the relationships of husbands and wives, parents and children, where sorrow, crying, pain, and death will be known no more.[5]

Although we don't know exactly what heaven will be like, we do know that the "same sociality which exists among us here will exist among us there, only it will be coupled with eternal glory, which glory we do not now enjoy" (Doctrine and Covenants 130:2).

So what will we *do* in the celestial kingdom? Author Anthony Sweat offers this answer:

> A youth group from a mainstream Christian denomination once visited the LDS seminary where I worked. They wanted to find out more about Latter-day Saint doctrines, so we had an open and cordial discussion where they asked me questions.
>
> At one point, one of them questioned the Church's doctrine on eternal families and becoming like God, to which I asked him, "Well, according to your church, what do you think you will do in heaven?"
>
> He thought for a second, and then said, "Worship God."
>
> I told him that was a faithful response, but I wanted him to explain more. "How will you worship him?" I asked.
>
> "By singing," he said.
>
> "Forever?" I asked. "What else will you do besides sing?"
>
> He was slightly puzzled and said, "Well, nothing . . . we'll just worship."
>
> I told him that I respected his answer, but believed that God had more in mind for His children than eternal songs. I told him that we believed that we came to earth to learn to become like our Heavenly Father. That those who qualify for exaltation will become like God, have eternal lives, eternal families, and eternal relationships. They will create, act, and move. They will progress in glory. Their eternal life will be an extension of all noble things of earthly life, only coupled with eternal glory. I told him we will also worship God in the next life, but we worship God by emulating and becoming like God through Jesus Christ.
>
> "That is how we believe we worship God. Doesn't that sound more exciting than just harps and singing?" I asked.

The Keys to the Celestial Kingdom

We testify that through the three degrees of glory, God "saves all the works of his hands" (Doctrine and Covenants 76:43). Our Father in Heaven and our Savior Jesus Christ are so kind and loving, and so merciful, that they will give all of their children an eternal inheritance in a degree of heaven. You don't have to settle for the telestial or terrestrial kingdoms though. If you make and keep sacred covenants with Jesus Christ, He will perfect you so that you can dwell with Him eternally in the celestial kingdom.

> We invite you to exercise faith in Christ, repent of your sins, and partake of the sacrament every Sunday to renew your baptismal covenants with Christ. Remember, continued faith, repentance, and making and keeping covenants are the keys to the celestial kingdom.

Still Have Questions?

Do I have to be married to go to the celestial kingdom?

Simply stated—no. The requirements to enter the celestial kingdom are faith in the Lord Jesus Christ, repentance, baptism by immersion, reception of the Holy Ghost, and enduring faithfully to the end (see Doctrine and Covenants 76:51–53). However, if we want to obtain the highest degree of the celestial kingdom (known as "exaltation"), we must have an eternal marriage sealed in the temple.

Doctrine and Covenants 131 teaches us that "in the celestial glory there are three heavens or degrees; and in order to obtain the highest, a man must enter into this order of the priesthood [meaning the new and everlasting covenant of marriage]; and if he does not, he cannot obtain it. He may enter into the other, but that is the end of his kingdom; he cannot have an increase" (Doctrine and Covenants 131:1–4).

What is the "unforgivable" sin that makes someone a "son of perdition"?

Some people worry that they might not receive any kingdom of glory, become a son of perdition and be cast to outer darkness. As a matter of fact, in one group who took our survey at the beginning of this chapter, 2 percent of them wrote in that they thought they would go to outer darkness.

To ease our worries, President Spencer W. Kimball taught, "The sin against the Holy Ghost requires such knowledge that it is manifestly impossible for the [average person] to commit such a sin."[6] And Joseph Smith said, "What must a man do to commit the unpardonable sin? He must receive the Holy Ghost, have the heavens opened unto him, and know God, and then sin against Him. . . . He has got to say that the sun does not shine while he sees it; he has got to deny Jesus Christ when the heavens have been opened unto him, and to deny the plan of salvation with his eyes open to the truth of it."[7]

What does it mean to "endure to the end"?

Sometimes we think that enduring to the end sounds painful, like it is not something to be enjoyed. President Henry B. Eyring said that when he first read of enduring to the end, he thought "it sounded grim, like sitting still and holding on to the arms of the chair while someone pulled out my tooth."[8]

Actually, we should think of it more as "abiding" or "staying in" the gospel, or "enduring in" the gospel, and not enduring *the gospel*. Enduring *in* the gospel brings happiness, love, joy, and peace. It is something to be enjoyed, not to get over with.

Teach the Plan!

Who Will Go to the Celestial Kingdom?

Objective: To help learners know about the three degrees of glory and understand what is required to qualify for eternal life in the celestial kingdom.

Attention Getter: Teach the Plan #1: Have each of your kids anonymously take the survey about which kingdom they think they would go to if they died and were judged today. Share with them the results of the poll of the EFY participants. Ask, "Why do you think the majority of youth don't think they will make it to the celestial kingdom?" Use this activity to lead into a discussion of what is really required to qualify for eternal life in the celestial kingdom.

Attention Getter: Teach the Plan #5. Have your kids add up the numbers for the words "hard work," "knowledge," and "attitude." Then show them the "love of God" answer and discuss with them why the love of God is necessary to make us perfect and to qualify us for the celestial kingdom. Use this as a springboard into a discussion on qualifying for the celestial kingdom.

Lesson Activity: Teach the Plan #2. Divide your family into three groups. Assign one group the celestial kingdom, one group the terrestrial kingdom, and one group the telestial kingdom. Ask each group to study the following verses from Doctrine and Covenants 76:

Celestial (vs. 50–70, 92–96)
Terrestrial (vs. 71–80, 91, 97)
Telestial (vs. 81–90, 98–112)

Have each group find the answers to the following two questions from their verses:

1. What are the characteristics of the people who go to this kingdom?
2. What is this kingdom like?

Have each group share with the others the answers to their questions related to their assigned kingdom.

Lesson Activity: Teach the Plan #4. Read Doctrine and Covenants 76:51–53 and highlight all the requirements that are necessary to qualify for the celestial kingdom. Discuss with your family what each qualification means and ask them if they are currently meeting all those requirements. If so, keep on the path! You're on the way! If not, what might need to change in your life?

Discussion Questions: The following questions may help your children in understanding, identifying, and applying some gospel truths related to qualifying for the celestial kingdom:

Teach the Plan #6: Ask, "What does it teach you about God and Jesus Christ to know that everybody born on earth (except the few sons of perdition) will go to a heaven? How might that truth change your perspective of eternity?"

Teach the Plan #3: Ask, "What do you think it means to be 'valiant in the testimony of Jesus' (see 2 Nephi 31:20; Moroni 10:32; James 1:22)? What does it look like to be valiant, or not valiant, in the testimony of Jesus?"

Invitation to Act: Live the Plan: Invite your children to exercise faith, repent, and renew their baptismal covenants this Sunday. Testify to them that those who continue in this righteous cycle of covenant making and renewing are on the path to the celestial kingdom.

16

What Will We Be like When We're Resurrected?

When we look in the mirror, most of us aren't 100 percent satisfied with what we see. Many of us wish we weren't so scrawny or so soft. Others might wish they were a little taller, tanned, or toned. We wish our teeth didn't need train tracks to be straight or were already snow white. We wish our skin was porcelain perfect and pimple-free. And all those split ends, really? All in all, most of us wish we were a little more beautiful or handsome—a little more physically perfect.

On a less superficial level, some of us aren't dealing with problems about how our bodies *look*, but with how our bodies *function*. Many people deal every day with diabetes, chronic fatigue, mental illness, liver failure, blindness, paralysis, or many other ailments. Although each of us have varying levels and types of physical problems, there is something deep down inside of us that longs for physical perfection—to be put together and functioning the way we were meant to. And guess what? One day, after this life, we will.

 Through Jesus' gift of the resurrection, God has promised each of us that "all things" with our bodies "shall be restored to their proper and perfect frame" (Alma 40:23; see also Alma 11:44; Doctrine and Covenants 138:17). What a blessing!

So what is the resurrection, why is it necessary, and how will it affect us individually? This chapter will answer some of those questions and many more.

Why Do We Need to Be Resurrected?

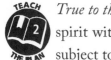 *True to the Faith* defines *resurrection* as "the reuniting of the spirit with the body in a perfect, immortal state, no longer subject to disease or death."[1]

Being resurrected is part of God's plan "to enable us to become like Him and receive a fulness of joy."[2] God the Father has an immortal "body of flesh and bones as tangible as man's" (Doctrine and Covenants 130:22), and so having a body of flesh and bone for our spirit contributes to our happiness.

Because we have bodies right now, we might not fully appreciate how great they are, and how much we will miss them when we don't have them anymore. Think about all we can do that brings us joy because of our bodies! The Lord has said that when our body and spirit are separated "man cannot receive a fulness of joy" (Doctrine and Covenants 93:33). In fact, the Lord has also said that when we are separated from our bodies in the spirit world it will seem like "bondage" (Doctrine and Covenants 45:17). However, when our body and spirit are eternally reconnected in the resurrection, we will "receive a fulness of joy" (Doctrine and Covenants 93:33), just as God desires for us. When we understand how joy comes from having our bodies, we realize that the resurrection is a marvelous blessing.

You are probably familiar with the "hand inside the glove" analogy of our spirit and body. If you aren't, then do this: Get a glove, put your hand inside of it, and wiggle your fingers and move the glove around. The glove is like our body, and the hand is like our spirit. When the spirit is in the body, there is life and movement. When you pull your hand out of the glove, the glove is lifeless—just like when the spirit leaves the body. Putting your hand back inside the glove is similar to the resurrection: the reuniting of the body and spirit.

However, one thing many people don't mention with this common analogy is that when our hand is outside the glove, we can still move and act and control the bare hand. So why do we even need the glove? Well, think of all the extra things we can do in life because of different types of gloves: we can play in the snow, catch a baseball, keep our hands sterile and clean, and take hot things out of the oven. Take a minute and think of as many different types of gloves as you can, and what they enable you to do that otherwise you couldn't.

Just like a glove can enhance our hands' ability, the benefit of a physical body of flesh and bones is that it allows us to be able to do things we otherwise could not if we remained only as disembodied spirits.

Resurrection Because of Christ

Perhaps the most important truth we must understand about the resurrection is that it is only possible through Jesus Christ. From His mortal mother, Mary, Jesus inherited the ability to die, and from His immortal Father, He received the power to overcome death. President Joseph Fielding Smith said, "Jesus was the *only person* who ever came into this world who had *power over death*."[3]

Jesus was the first person on this earth to be resurrected, and through His authority and power, all of mankind will also be resurrected (2 Nephi 2:8–9). The Book of Mormon explains why the Resurrection should fill our hearts with gratitude for the Savior: "For behold, if the flesh should rise no more our spirits must become subject to that angel who fell from before the presence of the Eternal God, and became the devil, to rise no more. And our spirits must have become like unto him, and we become devils, angels to a devil, to be shut out from the presence of our God" (2 Nephi 9:8–9). In other words, if it were not for the resurrection, not only could we never become like God, but we would also be doomed to live with the devil for eternity. Understanding the glory of the resurrection should fill our hearts with gratitude for the Savior, who makes the Resurrection possible.

Questions about the Resurrection

 Let's take a look at a few of the most frequently asked questions about the Resurrection.

Who Will Be Resurrected?

The Apostle Paul taught, "For as in Adam all die, even so in Christ shall all be made alive" (1 Corinthians 15:22). That's right, every single person who has ever lived on earth will be resurrected: the young and the old, the righteous and the wicked. *"Preach My Gospel"* says, "Every person born on earth will be resurrected because Jesus Christ overcame death."[4] Because of Jesus Christ, all of us—and all those who have died—will receive the free gift of resurrection.

Will Babies Be Resurrected as Babies?

Yes. However, they will eventually grow and develop into full resurrected adulthood. President Joseph Fielding Smith explained, "Children who die do not grow in the grave. They will come forth with their bodies as they were laid down and then they will grow to the full stature of manhood or womanhood after the resurrection."[5]

What Will I Look like after I Am Resurrected?

The simple answer is that we will look similar to what we look like now. We will still have two arms and two legs and be the same general person we are now. The prophet Amulek taught that "the spirit and the body shall be reunited again in its perfect form; both limb and joint shall be restored to its proper frame, even as we now are at this time" (Alma 11:43).

So we'll look like us—only better. Speaking of women, Elder

James E. Talmage said, "Mortal eye cannot see nor mind comprehend the beauty, glory, and majesty of a righteous woman made perfect in the celestial kingdom of God."[6] We're sure the same principle is true for men.

How Old Will I Be after I'm Resurrected?

The scriptures don't say what age we will be after we are resurrected, only that we will be in a proper, perfect form. President Spencer W. Kimball taught, "The body resurrected will be neither the unbalanced body of immature youth, nor the creaking, wrinkling one of many years, but when it is restored and resurrected it will undoubtedly return in the bloom of its greatest mortal perfection."[7]

Will I Be Able to Be Hurt or Die after I'm Resurrected?

No. The scriptures say that after someone is resurrected "they can die no more" (Alma 11:45). One interesting fact about resurrected bodies is that they have no blood in them. Heavenly Father and Jesus Christ have bodies of flesh and *bone,* not flesh and blood (see Doctrine and Covenants 130:22). Blood is a characteristic of mortal bodies (see Leviticus 17:14), not immortal, resurrected bodies. Joseph Smith taught that, in the resurrection, "the Spirit of god [will be] flowing in the [veins instead] of the blood."[8] If you stop and think of the symbolism of that truth, and about how Jesus Christ shed His blood for us, you can find some pretty cool insights.

What Happens to Our Physical Scars in the Resurrection?

President Joseph F. Smith taught, "Every organ, every limb that has been maimed, every deformity caused by accident or in any other way, will be restored and put right."[9]

Are All Resurrected Bodies the Same?

No. Not only are there three kingdoms of glory (celestial, terrestrial, and telestial), but there are also three different types of resurrected bodies. The Apostle Paul taught that there are "celestial bodies, and bodies terrestrial, and bodies telestial; but the glory of the celestial, one; and the terrestrial, another; and the telestial, another" (JST, 1 Corinthians 15:40). This means that there will be different types of bodies in the resurrection, some more glorious than others. We will be able to tell the difference between a celestial body and a telestial body just as easily as we can see the difference between a Ferrari and a Honda Accord.

President Joseph Fielding Smith explained, "In the resurrection there will be different kinds of bodies; they will not all be alike. The body a man receives will determine his place hereafter. There will be celestial bodies, terrestrial bodies, and telestial bodies, and these bodies will differ as distinctly as do bodies here."[10]

Will Everybody Be Resurrected at the Same Time?

No. The Savior taught that there will be different times that people are resurrected (see John 5:28–29). From Doctrine and Covenants 88:97–102, we learn that the righteous will be resurrected at the time of the Second Coming of Christ. This is often called "the morning of the first resurrection." Those spirits who will eventually go to the terrestrial kingdom will be resurrected sometime during the Millennium ("the afternoon of the first resurrection"), and those spirits who will go to the telestial kingdom will be resurrected at the end of the Millennium (the second resurrection).

What Can We Take with Us into the Resurrection?

This is a very important question because it highlights for us what we should focus on in this life. For example, since we can't take wealth with us into the next life, should we spend our time focusing on getting rich? Probably not. But Doctrine and Covenants 130:18–19 tells us, "Whatever principle of intelligence we attain unto in this life, it will rise with us in the resurrection. And if a person gains more knowledge and intelligence in this life through his diligence and obedience than another, he will have so much the advantage in the world to come." Focusing on gaining knowledge and intelligence should be a high priority.

We also learn from Doctrine and Covenants 132:7 that "all covenants, contracts, bonds" that are "sealed by the Holy Spirit of promise" continue in the next life. Thus, if we keep our covenants, our family relationships that have been sealed in the temple will continue after the resurrection. We should focus on our families and place our relationships with them as one of our highest priorities on earth.

We also take our character with us into the next life: If I am a kind person now, I'll be kind after the resurrection. If I love the gospel here, I'll love the gospel after the resurrection. The Book of Mormon teaches us that the "same spirit which doth possess your bodies at the time that ye go out of this life, that same spirit will have power to possess your body in that eternal world" (Alma 34:34). Thus, we should work on developing our Christlike attributes in this life, because they will go with us into the next life.

Will Animals Be Resurrected?

Yes. President Joseph Fielding Smith taught, "Every creature on the earth, whether it be man, *animal, fish, fowl,* or *other creature,* that the Lord has created, is *redeemed from death* on the *same terms* that man is redeemed"[11] (see also Doctrine and Covenants 29:23–25; 77:2). So yes, animals will be resurrected, but there is no scriptural evidence on whether you'll be able to be with your dog in the resurrection.

When Will People Be Resurrected If They Live during the Millennium?

The people who are alive during the Millennium will continue to grow until they are old and will then be instantaneously resurrected.

As we learn from the Doctrine and Covenants: "Wherefore, children shall grow up until they become old; old men shall die; but they shall not sleep in the dust, but they shall be changed in the twinkling of an eye" (Doctrine and Covenants 63:51).

What If I'm Afraid to Die?

The fear of dying is the tenth most common phobia.[12] But the righteous do not need to fear death. Proverbs 14:32 says, "The righteous [person] hath hope in his death." And President Joseph F. Smith said, "I rejoice that I am born to live, to die, and to live again. I thank God for this intelligence. It gives me joy and peace that the world cannot give, neither can the world take it away."[13] These quotes should fill our hearts with comfort; because of the glorious resurrection that awaits us, we do not need to fear death.

The Resurrection Will Be Glorious

We should look forward with great joy to the day of resurrection. Imagine never getting sick again, never being tired again, and never feeling pain again. Imagine all physical illnesses, deformities, and shortcomings going away. Imagine a physical body in a perfect, celestial form. Imagine living forever with those we love.

True to the Faith teaches, "An understanding and testimony of the resurrection can give you hope and perspective as you experience the challenges, trials, and triumphs of life. You can find comfort in the assurance that the Savior lives and that through His Atonement, 'he breaketh the bands of death, that the grave shall have no victory, and that the sting of death should be swallowed up in the hopes of glory' (Alma 22:14)."[14]

LIVE THE PLAN The resurrection is a glorious doctrine. Plan a short talk about the resurrection that could be used for a Duty to God or Personal Progress requirement. Use the Topical Guide to find some scriptures that you could use.

Teach the Plan!

What Will We Be like When We're Resurrected?

Objective: To help learners understand the nature and purpose of the resurrection.

Attention Getter: Teach the Plan #5. Ask your kids what their worst fear is. Tell your children that the fear of dying is one of people's top ten fears. (Download a list of the top ten phobias at http://seek.deseretbook.com/bigpicture.) Ask your family, "Why, if we believe in Jesus Christ, should we not fear death?"

Attention Getter: Teach the Plan #2. Ask your children to define "resurrection." Read the definition from *True to the Faith* and discuss what aspects they expressed that are similar.

Lesson Activity: Teach the Plan #4. Read the list of questions in the chapter to your children without giving the answers. Have them pick which question they are most interested in. Ask them to first tell you what they think the answer might be, then read to them the answers provided for each question.

Discussion Questions: The following questions may help your children in understanding, identifying, and applying some gospel truths related to the resurrection:

Teach the Plan #1: Ask, "What do you think a body in its 'perfect frame' looks and feels like?"

Teach the Plan #3: Ask, "Why do you think having a body of flesh and bone is necessary for a fullness of joy in the next life?"

Teach the Plan #6: Ask, "Why do you look forward to the resurrection?"

Invitation to Act: Live the Plan: Invite your family members to look up "resurrection" in the Topical Guide and study what the scriptures teach about the resurrection. Ask them to prepare a short talk on the subject of resurrection that could be given in church or used to pass off a Duty to God or Personal Progress requirement.

17

Our Final Judgment

In a memorable address in the Book of Mormon, Alma asks, "Can ye imagine yourselves brought before the tribunal of God?" (Alma 5:18). Think about that for a moment. Will Judgment Day be like a celestial courtroom with heavenly lawyers questioning us?

"Where were you on the night of April 16, 2011?"

"At home, reading my scriptures."

"Wrong! Introducing Exhibit A. Let's see what the *video* says!" And then there will be a recording of that night showing us doing some sinful deed and judgment will be executed. Ah, man!

Well, here's the good news: it probably won't be like that. ☺

Another way some people picture the Final Judgment is with God holding the scales of justice with one side labeled "good" and the other side labeled "bad."

We imagine that God will call us up before His throne and then show us of all the good and bad things we have done in our life, depositing a drop on the "good" or "bad" side of the scales each time we acted a certain way.

"Went to church—good." (Kerplink!)

"While at church, kicked your brother in the shin—bad." (Kerplunk!)

We think that if the good outweighs the bad, and the scale tips to the good side, then some celestial angel shouts, "We have a winner!" and off we go to the celestial kingdom.

Well, that's not how it will be either.

 So, what is the Final Judgment? Who will do the judging? What will it really be like? Here are some answers.

Intermediate Judgments and the Final Judgment

It is important to understand that the Final Judgment could really be called the Final *Placement,* or the *Eternal* Judgment— meaning the final placement in our eternal kingdoms (either celestial, terrestrial, or telestial).

The Final Judgment takes place *after* the resurrection (see Alma 11:41), and it is an acknowledgment and acceptance that all of God's "judgments are just" and "that he is just in all his works, and that he is merciful unto the children of men" (Alma 12:15). However, the Final Judgment is also the last of many intermediate judgments. God has, does, and will judge us at multiple times throughout our lives as we progress through the plan of salvation.

We were judged in the premortal existence and because we remained faithful to God's plan, we were deemed worthy to come to earth (see Abraham 3:26–28). We are judged when we die and enter the spirit world and are assigned to either spirit paradise or spirit prison (see Alma 40:11–14). We are judged at the Second Coming of Christ, whether we are righteous and will come forth in the morning of the first resurrection (celestial), or later in the terrestrial or telestial resurrections (see Doctrine and Covenants 88:97–102).

And, perhaps most common, we are judged by God each day of our lives whether we are faithful to His commandments, worthy of His Spirit (see Helaman 4:24), and qualified to receive of His blessings (see Doctrine and Covenants 130:20–21).

Who Will Do the Judging?

There are different ways to look at the Final Judgment. Ultimately, Jesus Christ is the final judge. He said, "For the Father judgeth no man, but hath committed all judgment unto the Son" (John 5:22). The Nephite prophet Jacob taught, "When all men . . . have become immortal, they must appear before the judgment-seat of the Holy One of Israel; and then cometh the judgment" (2 Nephi 9:15). Because of Jesus' Atonement, He alone is "the keeper of the gate" (2 Nephi 9:41) and judges who may enter the celestial kingdom of God. He alone has the authority to recommend and present those who qualify—by virtue of their covenants and faithfulness to Him—for eternal life with God (see Doctrine and Covenants 45:2–3).

In addition, judgment will take place by Jesus' Twelve Apostles. Nephi was told in a vision, "Thou rememberest the twelve apostles of the Lamb? Behold they are they who shall judge the twelve tribes of Israel" (1 Nephi 12:9). Other dispensation heads who have held keys of the priesthood, such as Joseph Smith, will also play a role in judgment.[1]

Interestingly, we will also judge ourselves. Alma taught that people "are their own judges" (Alma 41:7). Some of us might think, "Cool! If I can be my own judge, I'll just judge myself worthy of the celestial kingdom and walk right in." First of all, we can't sneak in (remember that verse about Jesus being the "keeper of the gate"?), but second of all, even if we could sneak in, we wouldn't. The prophet Moroni put it this way: "Do ye suppose that ye could be happy to dwell with that holy Being, when your souls are racked with a consciousness of guilt that ye have ever abused his laws? Behold, I say unto you that ye would be more miserable to dwell with a holy and just God, under a consciousness of your filthiness before him, than ye would to dwell with the damned souls in hell" (Mormon 9:3–4).

In other words, even if wicked people *could* get into heaven, they wouldn't want to, because they would feel so uncomfortable. It would be like going to prom in cutoffs and a T-shirt. We would feel out of place.

LDS author and speaker Brad Wilcox related this story that helps illustrate this point:

> I know a young man who just got out of prison—again. . . . When he was a teenager dealing with every bad habit a teenage boy can have, I said to his father, "We need to get him to EFY [Especially For Youth]." . . .
>
> His dad said, "I can't afford that."
>
> I said, "I can't afford it either, but you put some in, and I'll put some in. . . ."
>
> We finally got the kid to EFY, but how long do you think he lasted? Not even a day. By the end of the first day he called his mother and said, "Get me out of here!" Heaven will not be heaven for those who have not chosen to be heavenly. . . .
>
> . . . The older I get, and the more I understand this wonderful *plan of redemption,* the more I realize that in the final judgment it will *not* be the unrepentant sinner begging Jesus, "Let me stay." No, he will probably be saying, "Get me out of here!"[2]

We will not want to dwell in God's presence if we are not worthy to be there. However, "truth embraceth truth; virtue loveth virtue; [and] light cleaveth unto light" (Doctrine and Covenants 88:40). For those who have righteously followed Christ, they will feel perfectly at home in God's kingdom if they have become like Him and "received his image in [their] countenances" (Alma 5:14).

What Will We Be Judged On?

At the Final Judgment, we know that we will—in some way—account for our actions, words, and thoughts (see Alma 12:14). Regarding our works, the Apostle John said, "I saw the dead, small and great, stand before God; and the books were opened . . . and the dead were judged out of those things which were written in the books, according to their works" (Revelation 20:12).

The Savior taught, "Every *idle* word that men shall speak, they shall give an account thereof in the day of judgment" (Matthew 12:36; emphasis added), which should be motivation enough for all of us to watch the words we use and how we speak.

And Alma added that not only will we account for our words and deeds, but "our thoughts will also condemn us" (Alma 12:14), which is one more reason why we should strive to have clean thoughts.

Last, not only will we be judged based upon what we did, but also on what we *wanted* to do. The scriptures teach that—for good and for bad—"the Lord will judge all men according to their works, according to the *desire of their hearts*" (Doctrine and Covenants 137:9; emphasis added).

Before family home evening begins, assign one family member to take note of everything that somebody else does for five minutes. Be sure to tell them to do it secretly and to write down as much detail as possible. Partway through the lesson, announce that someone in the room has silently been taking notes of someone else concerning everything they said and did for the past five minutes.

Ask who would feel nervous if they were the person being watched? Who would worry if their actions were read out loud? Who would feel confident if it were read about them? Why? As long as it is appropriate (which it more than likely will be), read the comments and actions of the person out loud.

Have a discussion and ask "How is this like the Final Judgment? Based on what the scriptures and prophets have taught, how is this activity not like the Final Judgment?"

What Have We Become?

But the Final Judgment is more than just what we've done or said or thought; it is about what we've *become*. Elder Dallin H. Oaks taught: "The Final Judgment is not just an evaluation of a sum total of good and evil acts—what we have *done*. It is an acknowledgment of the final effect of our acts and thoughts—what we have *become*. It is not enough for anyone just to go through the motions. The commandments, ordinances, and covenants of the gospel are not a list of deposits required to be made in some heavenly account. The gospel of Jesus Christ is a plan that shows us how to become what our Heavenly Father desires us to become."[3]

Who we've *become* will be more important to God than what we have *done*. Metaphorically speaking, at the Judgment, God will open us up and take a look at our hearts. He will look to see if our character is Christlike, if our hearts are pure, and if we have charity and love (see Moroni 7:48). God will want to see if the person standing before Him has fulfilled the entire purpose of the plan of salvation, which is "to become like Him."[4]

Looking Forward to Judgment Day

The Final Judgment is something that will happen for everyone. All of us, at some point, "must come forth and stand before [God] in his glory, and in his power, and in his might, majesty, and dominion" (Alma 12:15). At the Final Judgment, we know that God will be just (see 2 Nephi 26:7). He will not throw His laws and requirements of faithfulness out the window, for He is a God of order, and a God of law, and that would not be fair or just for Him to do so (see Alma 42:22–25). We will not be able to hide from God (see Alma 12:14), or deceive him (see Alma 18:32), or escape our deserved fate (see Doctrine and Covenants 112:34). If our works have been evil and we haven't repented, we will receive a just punishment.

But we also know that Jesus "is a merciful Being, even unto salvation, to those who will repent and believe on his name" (Alma 26:35). Through the goodness, kindness, and love of God the Father has given to us through His Son Jesus Christ, we can and will receive mercy in spite of our imperfections. The prophet Lehi taught that Christ's "power, and goodness, and mercy are over all the inhabitants of the earth; and, because thou art merciful, thou wilt not suffer those who come unto thee that they shall perish!" (1 Nephi 1:14). In fact, the plan of salvation is often called "the plan of mercy" (Alma 42:15). Those who have come unto Christ and been perfected in Him (see Moroni 10:32) will not find justice at the judgment bar, but they will find and be claimed by mercy and salvation (see Alma 42:23–25).

President J. Reuben Clark Jr. said, "I feel that [God] will give that punishment which is the very least that our transgression will justify. . . . I believe that when it comes to making the rewards for our good conduct, he will give us the maximum that is possible to give."[5]

Sometimes Judgment Day has a negative connotation, like it is a day to be feared. However, if we have been disciples of Christ, made covenants with Him, and been born again by receiving of His Atonement, "then shall thy confidence wax strong in the presence of God" (Doctrine and Covenants 121:45). The Final Judgment can be like a homecoming and a graduation celebration, not a test and a trial. For those who have prepared themselves well through the Atonement of Christ, Judgment will be a glorious day—a day of reward and recompense for a faithful life of enduring to the end. A day when the Lord will say: "Come, ye blessed of my Father, inherit the kingdom prepared for you from the foundation of the world" (Matthew 25:34).

What Questions Will I Be Asked at the Final Judgment?

Speaking to a group of priesthood holders, President David O. Mckay said,

> Let me assure you, brethren, that someday you will have a personal priesthood interview with the Savior, himself. If you are interested, I will tell you the order in which He will ask you to account for your earthly responsibilities.
>
> First, He will request an accountability report about your relationship with your wife. Have you actively been engaged in making her happy and ensuring that her needs have been met as an individual?
>
> Second, He will want an accountability report about each of your children individually. He will not attempt to have this for simple family stewardship, but he will request information about your relationship to each and every child.
>
> Third, He will want to know what you personally have done with the talents that you were given in the pre-existence.
>
> Fourth, He will want a summary of your activity in your church assignments. He will not be necessarily interested in what assignments you have had, for in his eyes the home teacher and the mission president are probably equals, but he will request a summary of how you have been of service to your fellow men in your church assignments.
>
> Fifth, He will have no interest in how you earned your living, but if you were honest in all your dealings.
>
> Sixth, He will ask for an accountability on what you have done to contribute in a positive manner to your community, state, country and the world."[6]

Still Have Questions?

What should I do if I'm scared for the day of judgment?

REPENT! ☺

If you are scared for the day of judgment, take courage from this truth written by Nephi: "The righteous need not fear" (1 Nephi 22:22). If you are righteous, do not worry about the Judgment—it will be a great and glorious day. If there are specific things you are doing right now that you would be ashamed of at the day of judgment, then stop doing those things today and begin the process of repentance and change.

> **LIVE THE PLAN** Elder Dallin H. Oaks asked: "If we knew that we would meet the Lord tomorrow—through our premature death or through His unexpected coming—what would we do today? What confessions would we make? What practices would we discontinue? What accounts would we settle? What forgivenesses would we extend? What testimonies would we bear? If we would do those things then, why not now?"[7] We invite you to consider the things in your life which you want to make right before being judged by God, and we encourage you to act *today* on what comes to your mind.

What if I do something bad but repent? Will others find out at the last day?

One of the scary things (for the wicked) about the Judgment is that "the rebellious shall be pierced with much sorrow; for their iniquities shall be spoken upon the housetops, and their secret acts shall be revealed" (Doctrine and Covenants 1:3). However, that is only for the rebellious who haven't repented. In Doctrine and Covenants 58:42, Christ says, "He who has repented of his sins, the same is forgiven, and I, the Lord, remember them no more." If Christ no longer remembers the sin, it definitely won't be revealed at the last day. It's the sins we refuse to repent of that will be revealed at Judgment Day.

Teach the Plan!

Our Final Judgment

Objective: To help learners better prepare themselves for the Final Judgment.

Attention Getter: Experiment upon the Word: Record someone's actions in detail for five minutes. Reveal the findings to your kids and then ask, "How will this be like the Final Judgment? How will it not?" Use their answers to lead into a scriptural lesson on the Final Judgment.

Attention Getter: Teach the Plan #1. Invite your children to picture the Final Judgment and then ask them what they think it will be like. Will it be more like a courtroom proceeding where lawyers weigh the evidence—good or bad? Will it be more like a movie of our life that we can watch? Will it be more like a private interview with the bishop? Use their answers to lead you into a lesson on what the scriptures teach us about the Final Judgment.

Lesson Activity: Teach the Plan #2. Assign each member of your family a number—1, 2, or 3. Give them five minutes to discover as many scriptures as they can find to answer the corresponding questions below:

1. What is the Final Judgment?
2. Who will do the judging?
3. What will we be judged on?

Encourage them to use the Index and Topical Guide for help. Have each person share the scriptures he or she found that give insights to the question. After everyone has given their insights, read the answers provided in this chapter to check for validation, understanding, and additional truths.

Discussion Questions: The following questions may help your children in understanding, identifying, and applying some gospel truths related to the Final Judgment:

Teach the Plan #3: Ask, "Why is it both a good thing—and potentially a bad thing—that the Lord says He will judge us by not only our works, but by the desires of our hearts? In what ways might our desires and our works be related?"

Teach the Plan #4: Ask, "How does it change your view that what we have

done is less important to God than what we have *become*? How might that knowledge affect the things you do, and how you do them?"

Invitation to Act: Read the quote by Elder Dallin H. Oaks next to the Live the Plan icon. Invite your children to act on what comes to their minds after they consider the thought that they would meet the Lord tomorrow.

Conclusion

The Plan to Guide Our Everyday Lives

In this book we have covered most of the major areas of God's plan of salvation, from being foreordained in the premortal existence, to the creation of the world, to being born again, and many more. Some people might not see how learning about God's plan from the very beginning to the very end (things that have happened in the past, or that will happen in the future) applies to their everyday life right now. Thoughts might cross their minds like, "I can't think about *foreordination*—I need to focus on gaining an *education.* I don't need to know about being *born again*—I need to find a *job again.* I'm not concerned about the *creation*—I'm more interested in *flirtation!*"

Right?

Well . . . actually . . . wrong.

The fact is that the truth found in the plan of salvation can be the guiding key to helping us know how to act and behave in everyday life. For example, knowing about foreordination can greatly enhance our current efforts in education. Working on being born again just might help turn us into the kind of person who will get a job again. And knowing the truths about creation can definitely guide everyday flirtation. That's because the plan of salvation gives us eternal truths to inform our everyday behaviors.

For example, using the topic of creation, the scriptures teach us that "God created man in his own image" (Genesis 1:27) and that our physical body is created in the image of God. Therefore, we understand that our bodies are sacred and should be treated with respect.

Look how that truth about creation can inform how we behave today: We should take care of our body, not intentionally harm it, and be as healthy as possible. We should treat our body with respect. We should dress modestly. We shouldn't touch other people's bodies inappropriately.

Do you see how knowing about the truth of the creation guides multiple different behaviors, even including flirtation? If we take someone on a date, the truth that our bodies are created in God's image can guide us to know that we should dress properly, not do any crazy stunts to try to show off for our date, treat our date kindly, and so forth.

The same is true for all of the behaviors, actions, and decisions, and other issues we face here in mortality: If we know and believe the truths of the plan of salvation, those truths can and should inform us on how to behave in our everyday lives.

The Plan of Salvation Is Relevant for Today

The truths of the plan of salvation can also inform and guide us on some of the difficult issues of our day. Believe it or not, the plan of salvation has a lot to do with daily newspaper headlines. Let's take a brief look at some difficult social issues of our day and see how the doctrines of the plan of salvation can help inform us on some of these problems.

Abortion

Premortal existence: Understanding that we lived with God before we were born helps us realize that a person does not abort a mere "fetus," but it is the body of a spirit child of God that is being aborted.

God created the world so that we could come to earth and gain a body. Abortion impedes the opportunity for a spirit child of God to come to earth to receive a body and progress in God's plan.

Agency: The prophets teach that "while you are free to choose your course of action, you are not free to choose the consequences."[1] Some deceptive arguments focus on a woman's right to choose to have an abortion. However, this viewpoint ignores the fact that the couple already has made choices (for example, the choice to have unprotected sexual relations), and ignores the fact that the couple has other choices that do not take away a human life (for example, the choice of working toward a marriage if possible, or pursuing an adoption plan if a stable marriage is not feasible).

Eternal life: Eternal life is living forever with God and becoming like Him. Children are created by God, and He loves them. Jesus said, "Suffer the little children to come unto me, and forbid them not: for of such is the kingdom of God" (Mark 10:14). Abortion is inconsistent with these truths.

Sexual Purity

Creation: We are created in God's image. Therefore, our bodies are sacred and should not be misused or mistreated, nor should we misuse or mistreat the bodies of others. Sexual relations outside of marriage misuses someone else's body, usually for selfish purposes. Additionally, sexual relations are closely tied to the biological power to create life. When we misuse our power to create life by having sex outside of the marriage covenant, we are misusing the Godlike power to create life.

The Atonement: Jesus Christ died for each one of us to save our souls. Elder Jeffrey R. Holland explained that breaking the law of chastity "abuses the very soul of that individual [and] desecrates the Atonement of Christ, which saved that soul."[2]

The family: Illicit sexual relations outside of marriage contribute to adultery, divorce, disease, abortion, neglect, poverty, and many other threats to the family. On the other hand, sexual purity protects and strengthens marriages and families, which are central to God's plan of happiness.

The degrees of glory: Those who misuse the Godlike power to create life will not be permitted to live with God, because they have not become like God. The scriptures teach that unrepentant breakers of the law of chastity will not go to the celestial kingdom (see 1 Corinthians 6:9; Doctrine and Covenants 76:99–106).

Same-Gender Marriage

Eternal life/Purpose of the plan: Anything that is inconsistent with God's plan of salvation for His children is not endorsed by the Lord. We believe that we are all the spirit children of "heavenly parents"[3]—of an eternal *Father and Mother* in heaven. The primary purpose of God's plan for us is to become more like them. Therefore, The Church of Jesus Christ of Latter-day Saints "affirms that marriage between a man and a woman is essential to the Creator's plan for the eternal destiny of his children."[4] Only a marriage between a man and a woman can enable a couple to become like our heavenly parents.

Creation: The scriptures say that God created woman from the rib of man (see Moses 3:22). This metaphor teaches us the reality that ultimately a man is incomplete without a woman, and a woman without a man (see 1 Corinthians 11:11). The prophets also teach us, "The nature of male and female spirits is such that they complete each other. Men and women are intended to progress together toward exaltation."[5]

Marriage and family: Marriage is closely tied to the biological powers to create children and form a family. A same-gender relationship is inconsistent with the begetting of children, as two people of the same gender cannot produce children.

Agency: Some people say that they have a natural inclination to same-gender attraction and so they can't control their behavior. However, this is inconsistent with the doctrine of agency. We know that we have the power to control our actions. Elder Dallin H. Oaks explained:

> Homosexual feelings are controllable. . . .
>
> . . . Feelings can be controlled and behavior can be controlled. . . .
>
> . . . We do not accept the fact that conditions that prevent people from attaining their eternal destiny were born into them without any ability to control. That is contrary to the plan of salvation, and it is contrary to the justice and mercy of God.[6]

The Plan of Salvation Can Change Our Lives Forever

We've looked at only three issues, but there are countless ways that the truths of the plan of salvation can apply to our everyday lives. Issues such as premature steady dating, swearing, cheating in school, or the importance of modesty and of serving a mission can directly be connected to the plan of salvation.

Try this experiment: Take a newspaper or a magazine and read through the articles, specifically looking for how the current events of the day can be related to gospel doctrines. What lessons can you learn? How can what you know about the plan of salvation help give you eternal perspective and truth to face the daily issues of life?

> **LIVE THE PLAN** Choose an issue that is important to you, or one that you or your friends perhaps struggle with—for example, swearing, cheating, pornography, or following the Word of Wisdom. Analyze the issue through the lens of several of the different doctrines we have discussed in this book. How do these truths help you better understand this issue?

As we follow a pattern of making life decisions based on the plan of salvation, it will literally change our life and bless us forever. Elder M. Russell Ballard promised, "Making life's decisions based on our Heavenly Father's plan is so important. If we truly believe that we are his children and are here on earth to learn to live, by faith, the teachings and the commandments of God and his Only Begotten Son, Jesus Christ, we will make the choices that will qualify us to one day return to live in their presence."[7]

Conclusion

TEACH 4 THE PLAN We testify of the truth of God's "great plan of happiness" (Alma 42:8). We know that as God's literal children, each of us here on earth has a divine nature and destiny. When we look at our lives from an eternal perspective, we see that our time on this earth is but a brief moment. The scriptures say that this "life . . . is even a vapour, that appeareth for a little time, and then vanisheth away" (James 4:14). However, our short time on earth has eternal consequences depending on how we choose to spend our mortal time. On the hinge of mortality swings the door of eternity.

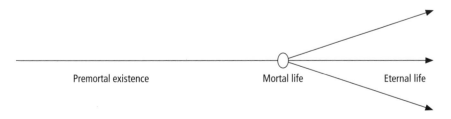

Premortal existence   Mortal life   Eternal life

Therefore, let us faithfully learn and follow God's great plan. Above all, let's follow our exemplar in the plan, Jesus Christ, and come unto Him by making and keeping covenants and following His teachings.

We testify that Jesus Christ is "the way, the truth, and the life" (John 14:6) and the only way to fulfill the purpose of the plan. We followed Jesus once (in our first estate in the premortal existence); let us follow Him again here in our second, earthly estate—for He is "mighty to save" (Alma 7:14).

And, because we love our Heavenly Father, let us worship God the best way possible: By following His plan, fulfilling our divine potential, and eventually becoming like God (see Romans 8:16–17).

We testify that such is possible—that as God's children and because of His divine plan of salvation, we truly can "become like Him and receive a fulness of joy."[8] As we implement God's plan in our lives, and share this plan with others, we too will know this great joy.

Teach the Plan!

The Plan to Guide Our Everyday Lives

Objective: To help learners better understand how the truths of the plan of salvation can be used to guide their everyday lives.

Attention Getter: Teach the Plan #2. Show an image of a person doing a risky activity and ask your family if they can figure out how the doctrine of the creation might have helped that person make a better choice.

Lesson Activity: Teach the Plan #3. Introduce the three societal issues mentioned—abortion, sexual purity, and same-gender marriage—and have your family discuss which gospel truths from the plan of salvation they feel best inform the issue at hand. Begin with the topic of abortion, and discuss your insights together. Do the same for the remaining two issues. Compare your answers to the possible answers provided in this chapter.

Lesson Activity: Experiment upon the Word: Gather a number of local newspapers or weekly magazines. Give each member of your family a section of the newspaper or a magazine. Ask them to find two or three issues mentioned in their newspaper or magazine and then decide which truths of the plan of salvation could be used to better inform the issue in question. Let each person share what he or she finds.

Discussion Question: Teach the Plan #1. Ask, "Why do you think some people turn to friends, societal trends, self-help books, professional opinions, findings from scientific studies, and other sources to look for guidance instead of turning to the truths of the plan of salvation? When is it okay to let these 'other' sources of information guide our lives, and when is it not?"

Visual: Show the image next to Teach the Plan #4. What other captions for this image might you come up with for this truth? What other metaphors or images might you use instead of this one?

Invitation to Act: Extend the "Live the Plan" invitation to your family. Choose an issue that is important to you and analyze it through the lens of the plan of salvation. How do the truths of the plan of salvation help you better understand this issue?

Notes

INTRODUCTION: THE "BIG PICTURE" OF THE PLAN OF SALVATION

1. Boyd K. Packer, *Mine Errand from the Lord* (Salt Lake City: Deseret Book, 2008), 3.
2. *"Preach My Gospel"* (Salt Lake City: The Church of Jesus Christ of Latter-day Saints, 2004), 48.
3. The illustrations of the plan of salvation found on pages 2, 3, and 4 are modeled after the illustrations found in *Old Testament Teacher Resource Manual* (Salt Lake City: The Church of Jesus Christ of Latter-day Saints, 2003), 18–19.
4. Bruce R. McConkie, *Sermons and Writings of Bruce R. McConkie,* ed. Mark L. McConkie (Salt Lake City: Bookcraft, 1989), 175.
5. Joseph F. Smith, *Teachings of Presidents of the Church: Joseph F. Smith* (Salt Lake City: The Church of Jesus Christ of Latter-day Saints, 1998), 337.
6. Lorenzo Snow, *The Teachings of Lorenzo Snow,* ed. Clyde J. Williams (Salt Lake City: Bookcraft, 1984), 1.
7. Joseph Smith, *Teachings of the Prophet Joseph Smith,* comp. Joseph Fielding Smith (Salt Lake City: Deseret Book, 1976), 324.
8. McConkie, *Sermons and Writings of Bruce R. McConkie*, 291.
9. See *Encyclopedia of Mormonism,* ed. Daniel H. Ludlow, 5 vols. (New York: Macmillan, 1992), 1:462; see also "I Am a Child of God," in *Children's Songbook* (Salt Lake City: The Church of Jesus Christ of Latter-day Saints, 1989), 2.

CHAPTER 1: OUR FIRST CHILDHOOD

1. Joseph F. Smith, *Teachings of Presidents of the Church: Joseph F. Smith* (Salt Lake City: The Church of Jesus Christ of Latter-day Saints, 1998), 331–32.
2. Ezra Taft Benson, "Jesus Christ—Gifts and Expectations," in *Speeches of the Year 1974* (Provo: Brigham Young University Press, 1975), 313.
3. *True to the Faith* (Salt Lake City: The Church of Jesus Christ of Latter-day Saints, 2004), 116.

4. Joseph Fielding Smith, *Doctrines of Salvation: Sermons and Writings of Joseph Fielding Smith,* ed. Bruce R. McConkie, 3 vols. (Salt Lake City: Bookcraft, 1954–56), 1:58–59.

5. Bruce R. McConkie, *The Mortal Messiah,* 4 vols. (Salt Lake City: Deseret Book, 1979–81), 1:23, 25.

6. *For the Strength of Youth* (Salt Lake City: The Church of Jesus Christ of Latter-day Saints, 2011), 3.

7. Richard G. Scott, "First Things First," *Ensign,* May 2001, 6.

8. Spencer W. Kimball, *Teachings of Presidents of the Church: Spencer W. Kimball* (Salt Lake City: The Church of Jesus Christ of Latter-day Saints, 2006), 3.

9. "The Family: A Proclamation to the World," *Ensign,* November 1995, 102.

10. Smith, *Doctrines of Salvation,* 1:61.

Chapter 2: The Creation of Our World

1. Richard G. Scott, "Truth: The Foundation of Correct Decisions," *Ensign,* November 2007, 90–91.

2. Joseph Smith, *Teachings of the Prophet Joseph Smith,* comp. Joseph Fielding Smith (Salt Lake City: Deseret Book, 1976), 181.

3. *For the Strength of Youth* (Salt Lake City: The Church of Jesus Christ of Latter-day Saints, 2011), 6.

4. Howard W. Hunter, *The Teachings of Howard W. Hunter,* ed. Clyde J. Williams (Salt Lake City: Bookcraft, 1997), 259.

5. Dieter F. Uchtdorf, "Happiness, Your Heritage," *Ensign,* November 2008, 118.

6. Neal A. Maxwell, "Our Creator's Cosmos," address delivered at the Twenty-Sixth Annual Church Education System Religion Educators Conference on August 13, 2002, at Brigham Young University, as cited by Richard Neitzel Holzapfel and Kent P. Jackson, eds., in *By Study and by Faith: Selections from the Religious Educator* (Provo, Utah: Religious Studies Center, Brigham Young University, 2009), 47.

7. Gordon B. Hinckley, "Our Responsibility to Our Young Women," *Ensign,* September 1988, 11.

8. First Presidency Minutes, April 7, 1931, as cited in *Encyclopedia of Mormonism,* Daniel H. Ludlow, ed., 4 vols. (New York: Macmillan, 1992), 2:478.

9. *Hymns of The Church of Jesus Christ of Latter-day Saints* (Salt Lake City: The Church of Jesus Christ of Latter-day Saints, 1985), no. 284.

10. See http://www.thefreedictionary.com/hie.

Chapter 3: The War in Heaven

1. "The Family: A Proclamation to the World," *Ensign,* November 1995, 102; emphasis added.

2. J. Reuben Clark Jr., *Behold the Lamb of God* (Salt Lake City: Deseret Book, 1962), 17.

3. See Neal A. Maxwell, "Wisdom and Order," *Ensign*, June 1994, 41–43.

4. See Clyde J. Williams, "The Book of Mormon and Overcoming Satan," in *Doctrines of the Book of Mormon: 1991 Sperry Symposium on the Book of Mormon* (Salt Lake City: Deseret Book, 1992), 244.

5. Bruce R. McConkie, *Mormon Doctrine,* 2d ed. (Salt Lake City: Bookcraft, 1966), 192.

6. *True to the Faith* (Salt Lake City: The Church of Jesus Christ of Latter-day Saints, 2004), 116.

7. "A testimony is to be *found* in the *bearing* of it!" Boyd K. Packer, "The Candle of the Lord," *Ensign*, January 1983, 54; emphasis in original.

8. Joseph Smith, *Teachings of the Prophet Joseph Smith,* comp. Joseph Fielding Smith (Salt Lake City: Deseret Book, 1976), 181.

9. Ezra Taft Benson, Church Educational System Devotional, Anaheim, California, February 8, 1987.

10. Neal A. Maxwell, *Faith in Every Footstep Instructor's Guide,* Church Educational System manual, 1996, 14.

CHAPTER 4: FOREORDAINED FOR GREATNESS

1. *True to the Faith* (Salt Lake City: The Church of Jesus Christ of Latter-day Saints, 2004), 69; emphasis added.

2. Ezra Taft Benson, "To the Young Women of the Church," *Ensign*, November 1986, 81.

3. *For the Strength of Youth* (Salt Lake City: The Church of Jesus Christ of Latter-day Saints, 2011), iii.

4. Joseph Smith, *Teachings of the Prophet Joseph Smith,* comp. Joseph Fielding Smith (Salt Lake City: The Church of Jesus Christ of Latter-day Saints, 1976), 365.

5. David A. Bednar, "Teach Them to Understand," Ricks College Campus Education Week Devotional, June 4, 1998; http://www2.byui.edu /Presentations/Transcripts/EducationWeek/1998_06_04.bednar.htm.

6. Neal A. Maxwell, "The Women of God," *Ensign*, May 1978, 10.

7. Sheri L. Dew, "Are We Not All Mothers?" *Ensign*, November 2001, 96; see also Spencer W. Kimball, "The Role of Righteous Women," *Ensign*, November 1979, 102–4.

8. Joseph F. Smith, *Teachings of Presidents of the Church: Joseph F. Smith* (Salt Lake City: The Church of Jesus Christ of Latter-day Saints, 1998), 152.

9. *True to the Faith,* 69.

10. Brigham Young, *Teachings of Presidents of the Church: Brigham Young* (Salt Lake City: The Church of Jesus Christ of Latter-day Saints, 1997), 52.

11. Joseph Fielding Smith, *The Way to Perfection* (Salt Lake City: Deseret Book, 1975), 44–45.

CHAPTER 5: HOW THE FALL OF ADAM AND EVE AFFECTS US ALL

1. Ezra Taft Benson, "The Book of Mormon and the Doctrine and Covenants," *Ensign*, May 1987, 83; emphasis added.

2. *Gospel Fundamentals* (Salt Lake City: The Church of Jesus Christ of Latter-day Saints, 1992), 25–26.

3. *Gospel Principles* (Salt Lake City: The Church of Jesus Christ of Latter-day Saints, 2009), 27.

4. Joseph Fielding Smith, in *Doctrines of the Gospel Student Manual, Religion 430 and 431* (Salt Lake City: CES Publishing, 2004), 20.

5. *Gospel Fundamentals*, 26.

6. *Gospel Fundamentals*, 26–27.

7. *True to the Faith* (Salt Lake City: The Church of Jesus Christ of Latter-day Saints, 2004), 57.

8. David A. Bednar, "Things as They Really Are," *Ensign*, June 2010, 17.

CHAPTER 6: WHAT IS THE PURPOSE OF OUR LIFE?

1. Joseph Smith, *History of The Church of Jesus Christ of Latter-day Saints*, 7 vols., edited by B. H. Roberts (Salt Lake City: The Church of Jesus Christ of Latter-day Saints, 1932–1951), 6:305.

2. *Lectures on Faith* (Salt Lake City: Deseret Book, 1985), 38; emphasis in original.

3. "The Family: A Proclamation to the World," *Ensign*, November 1995, 102.

4. David A. Bednar, "Things as They Really Are," *Ensign*, June 2010, 18.

5. Joseph Smith, *Teachings of the Prophet Joseph Smith*, comp. Joseph Fielding Smith (Salt Lake City: Deseret Book, 1976), 181; emphasis added.

6. Dallin H. Oaks, "Powerful Ideas," *Ensign*, November 1995, 25.

7. *For the Strength of Youth* (Salt Lake City: The Church of Jesus Christ of Latter-day Saints, 2011), 9–10.

8. *For the Strength of Youth*, 9.

9. John A. Widtsoe, *Evidences and Reconciliations*, 3 vol. (Salt Lake City: Bookcraft, 1987), 1:16–17.

10. David O. McKay, "Emotional Maturity," *The Instructor*, September 1959, 281.

11. Marion G. Romney, "The Celestial Nature of Self-Reliance," *Ensign*, November 1982, 93.

12. "The Family: A Proclamation to the World," 102.

13. Julie B. Beck, "Teaching the Doctrine of the Family," Seminaries and Institutes of Religion Satellite Broadcast, August 4, 2009, 2–3.

14. Richard G. Scott, "Truth Restored," *Ensign*, November 2005, 78.

15. Howard W. Hunter, "Follow the Son of God," *Ensign*, November 1994, 88.

16. Richard G. Scott, "First Things First," *Ensign*, May 2001, 7.

17. Boyd K. Packer, "The Choice," *Ensign*, November 1980, 21.

18. A. Theodore Tuttle, "The Things That Matter Most," *Ensign*, December 1971, 90.

Chapter 7: Agency

1. David O. McKay, *Teachings of Presidents of the Church: David O. McKay* (Salt Lake City: The Church of Jesus Christ of Latter-day Saints, 2003), 206.

2. Guide to the Scriptures, "Agency," scriptures.lds.org.

3. *Gospel Principles* (Salt Lake City: The Church of Jesus Christ of Latter-day Saints, 2009), 20.

4. Robert D. Hales, "To Act for Ourselves: The Gift and Blessings of Agency," *Ensign*, May 2006, 6.

5. *For the Strength of Youth* (Salt Lake City: The Church of Jesus Christ of Latter-day Saints, 2011), 2.

6. *For the Strength of Youth*, 2.

7. Paul V. Johnson, "Understanding and Living Gospel Doctrines," CES Satellite Training Broadcast, August 2003; http://si.lds.org/library/talks/training -broadcast/understanding-and-living-gospel-doctrines?lang=eng.

8. Harold B. Lee, "A Sure Trumpet Sound: Quotations from President Lee," *Ensign*, February 1974, 78.

9. Thomas S. Monson, "School Thy Feelings, O My Brother," *Ensign*, November 2009, 68; emphasis in original.

10. David A. Bednar, "And Nothing Shall Offend Them," *Ensign*, November 2006, 90; emphasis in original.

11. Lynn G. Robbins, "Finding Your Sweetheart," address given at BYU–Idaho, February 12, 2002; http://www2.byui.edu/Presentations/Transcripts /Devotionals/2002_02_12_Robbins.htm.

12. Viktor Frankl, *Man's Search for Meaning* (New York: Washington Square Press, 1984), 86.

13. *For the Strength of Youth*, 2.

14. Richard G. Scott, "He Lives," *Ensign*, November 1999, 87.

Chapter 8: God's Greatest Gift

1. *Hymns of The Church of Jesus Christ of Latter-day Saints* (Salt Lake City: The Church of Jesus Christ of Latter-day Saints, 1985), no. 98.

2. *True to the Faith* (Salt Lake City: The Church of Jesus Christ of Latter-day Saints, 2004), 15.

3. Boyd K. Packer, "'The Touch of the Master's Hand,'" *Ensign,* May 2001, 23–24; emphasis added and in original.

4. Henry B. Eyring, "Do Not Delay," *Ensign,* November 1999, 34.

5. D. Todd Christofferson, "Always Remember Him," Devotional at BYU–Idaho, January 27, 2009, http://www.byui.edu/Presentations/Transcripts /Devotionals/2009_01_27_Christofferson.htm.

6. Anne Perkins, "I Felt Broken," *New Era,* July 2006, 9; emphasis in original.

7. Merrill J. Bateman, "The Power to Heal from Within," *Ensign,* May 1995, 14.

8. David A. Bednar, "'In the Strength of the Lord,'" BYU Devotional, October 23, 2001, http://speeches.byu.edu/reader/reader.php?id=789.

9. Bible Dictionary, s.v. "grace," 697.

10. *True to the Faith,* 78.

11. Gordon B. Hinckley, "Let Us Live the Gospel More Fully," *Ensign,* November 2003, 103.

12. Bednar, "'In the Strength of the Lord.'"

13. *True to the Faith,* 77.

CHAPTER 9: CONNECTED TO CHRIST BY COVENANTS

1. *True to the Faith* (Salt Lake City: The Church of Jesus Christ of Latter-day Saints, 2004), 44.

2. See James E. Talmage, *Articles of Faith* (Salt Lake City: Deseret Book, 1984), 216.

3. *True to the Faith,* 170.

4. Boyd K. Packer, "The Holy Temple," *Ensign,* February 1995, 32.

5. *True to the Faith,* 171–72.

6. Gordon B. Hinckley, *Teachings of Gordon B. Hinckley* (Salt Lake City: Deseret Book, 1997), 148.

7. *Preparing to Enter the Holy Temple* (Salt Lake City: The Church of Jesus Christ of Latter-day Saints, 2002), 35.

8. David A. Bednar, "Honorably Hold a Name and Standing," *Ensign,* May 2009, 98.

9. Boyd K. Packer, "Covenants," *Ensign,* May 1987, 24.

10. D. Todd Christofferson, "The Power of Covenants," *Ensign,* May 2009, 20.

11. *True to the Faith,* 5–6.

CHAPTER 10: BEING BORN . . . AGAIN

1. Dallin H. Oaks, "Have You Been Saved?" *Ensign,* May 1998, 56.

2. David A. Bednar, "Ye Must Be Born Again," *Ensign,* May 2007, 20.

3. Bruce R. McConkie, *Mormon Doctrine*, 2d ed. (Salt Lake City: Bookcraft, 1966), 677; emphasis in original.

4. Dallin H. Oaks, "The Challenge to Become," *Ensign*, November 2000, 33; emphasis added.

5. Bednar, "Ye Must Be Born Again," 21.

6. *True to the Faith* (Salt Lake City: The Church of Jesus Christ of Latter-day Saints, 2004), 43.

7. Oaks, "The Challenge to Become," 32; emphasis added.

8. *True to the Faith*, 41.

9. Ezra Taft Benson, "A Mighty Change of Heart," *Ensign*, October 1989, 5.

10. D. Todd Christofferson, "Born Again," *Ensign*, May 2008, 78.

11. George Q. Cannon, in *Millennial Star* (April 23, 1894): 260.

12. See http://wiki.answers.com/Q/What_must_happen_to_coal_to_become_a _diamond.

Chapter 11: The Family

1. "The Family: A Proclamation to the World," *Ensign*, November 1995, 102.

2. *Family Guidebook* (Salt Lake City: The Church of Jesus Christ of Latter-day Saints, 2006), 1.

3. Bruce R. McConkie, in Conference Report, October 1955, 13.

4. J. E. McCulloch, quoted by David O. McKay, in Conference Report, April 1964, 5.

5. Julie B. Beck, "Teaching the Doctrine of the Family," *Ensign*, March 2011, 15.

6. *For the Strength of Youth* (Salt Lake City: The Church of Jesus Christ of Latter-day Saints, 2011), 35.

7. Recollection of Jesse W. Crosby, as cited in *The Teachings of Joseph Smith*, edited by Larry E. Dahl and Donald Q. Cannon (Salt Lake City: Bookcraft, 1997), 412.

8. David A. Bednar, "Marriage Is Essential to His Eternal Plan," Worldwide Leadership Training Meeting: Supporting the Family, February 11, 2006, *Ensign*, June 2006, 83–84.

9. *For the Strength of Youth*, 14.

10. Ezra Taft Benson, "To the Young Women of the Church," *Ensign*, November 1986, 81.

11. Richard G. Scott, "First Things First," *Ensign*, May 2001, 7; emphasis in original.

12. *Handbook 2: Administering the Church* (Salt Lake City: The Church of Jesus Christ of Latter-day Saints, 2010), 4.

13. Boyd K. Packer, "The Father and the Family," *Ensign*, May 1994, 19.

14. *True to the Faith* (Salt Lake City: The Church of Jesus Christ of Latter-day Saints, 2004), 49.
15. *True to the Faith*, 50.
16. Dallin H. Oaks, "The Great Plan of Happiness," *Ensign,* November 1993, 75.
17. "The Family: A Proclamation to the World," 102.
18. *Handbook 2: Administering the Church*, 196.
19. *Handbook 2: Administering the Church*, 196.
20. Richard G. Scott, "A Sure Witness of Jesus Christ: Elder Richard G. Scott," http://www.lds.org/study/prophets-speak-today/unto-all-the-world/sure -witness-elder-scott?lang=eng.

Chapter 12: Christ's Return to Earth

1. Joseph Fielding Smith, *Doctrines of Salvation: Sermons and Writings of Joseph Fielding Smith,* ed. Bruce R. McConkie, 3 vols. (Salt Lake City: Bookcraft, 1954–56), 3:1; emphasis in original and added.
2. Dallin H. Oaks, "Preparation for the Second Coming," *Ensign,* May 2004, 9.
3. *True to the Faith* (Salt Lake City: The Church of Jesus Christ of Latter-day Saints, 2004), 161.
4. Oaks, "Preparation for the Second Coming," 10.
5. Joseph Smith, *History of The Church of Jesus Christ of Latter-day Saints,* 7 vols. ed. B. H. Roberts (Salt Lake City: The Church of Jesus Christ of Latter-day Saints, 1932–51), 6:254.
6. *For the Strength of Youth* (Salt Lake City: The Church of Jesus Christ of Latter-day Saints, 2011), iii.
7. Boyd K. Packer, "Counsel to Youth," *Ensign,* November 2011, 19.

Chapter 13: A Thousand Years of Peace

1. *Gospel Fundamentals* (Salt Lake City: The Church of Jesus Christ of Latter-day Saints, 1992), 209.
2. Joseph Smith, *Teachings of the Prophet Joseph Smith,* comp. Joseph Fielding Smith (Salt Lake City: Deseret Book, 1976), 268.
3. *Gospel Fundamentals*, 209.
4. *Gospel Principles* (Salt Lake City: The Church of Jesus Christ of Latter-day Saints, 2009), 265.
5. Joseph Fielding Smith, *Church History and Modern Revelation* (Salt Lake City: Deseret Book, 1953), 1:192.
6. Spencer W. Kimball, *The Teachings of Spencer W. Kimball,* ed. Edward L. Kimball (Salt Lake City: Bookcraft, 1982), 172.
7. *Gospel Fundamentals*, 189.

8. Bruce R. McConkie, *Mormon Doctrine,* 2d ed. (Salt Lake City: Bookcraft, 1966), 211.

9. *Encyclopedia of Mormonism,* 4 vols., ed. Daniel H. Ludlow (New York: Macmillan, 1992), 2:432.

10. *Gospel Principles,* 267; see also Brigham Young, in *Teachings of Presidents of the Church: Brigham Young* (Salt Lake City: The Church of Jesus Christ of Latter-day Saints, 1997), 333–34.

11. McConkie, *Mormon Doctrine,* 496–97.

12. Bruce R. McConkie, *Millennial Messiah* (Salt Lake City: Deseret Book, 1982), 661.

13. *True to the Faith* (Salt Lake City: The Church of Jesus Christ of Latter-day Saints, 2004), 104.

14. Joseph Fielding Smith, *Doctrines of Salvation: Sermons and Writings of Joseph Fielding Smith,* ed. Bruce R. McConkie, 3 vols. (Salt Lake City: Bookcraft, 1954–56), 1:86.

15. *Gospel Principles,* 263.

16. *Gospel Principles,* 263.

17. *True to the Faith,* 104.

18. Brigham Young, in *Journal of Discourses,* 26 vols. (Liverpool: Latter-day Saints' Book Depot, 1854–86), 15:139.

19. *Gospel Principles,* 267.

CHAPTER 14: WHAT HAPPENS WHEN WE DIE?

1. See "World Vital Events," http://www.census.gov/population/international /data/idb/worldvitalevents.php.

2. Adapted from "The Big Religion Chart," http://www.religionfacts.com/big _religion_chart.htm.

3. George Q. Cannon, *Gospel Truth: Discourses and Writings of President George Q. Cannon,* arranged and ed. Jerreld L. Newquist (Salt Lake City: Zion's Book Store, 1957), 77–78.

4. *Gospel Principles* (Salt Lake City: The Church of Jesus Christ of Latter-day Saints, 2009), 244.

5. *True to the Faith* (Salt Lake City: The Church of Jesus Christ of Latter-day Saints, 2004), 46–47.

6. Ezra Taft Benson, "Life Is Eternal," *Ensign,* June 1971, 33.

7. Brigham Young, *Discourses of Brigham Young,* ed. John A. Widtsoe (Salt Lake City: Deseret Book, 1954), 376; emphasis added.

8. *Gospel Principles,* 242.

9. Brigham Young, in *Teachings of Presidents of the Church: Brigham Young* (Salt Lake City: The Church of Jesus Christ of Latter-day Saints, 1997), 273.

10. *Gospel Fundamentals* (Salt Lake City: The Church of Jesus Christ of Latter-day Saints, 1992), 213.

11. *Gospel Principles*, 242.

12. Charles W. Penrose, in *Journal of Discourses*, 26 vols. (Liverpool: Latter-day Saints' Book Depot, 1854–86), 26:22.

13. *Gospel Principles*, 241.

14. Hartman Rector Jr., in Conference Report, October 1970, 74.

15. Russell M. Nelson, "Addiction or Freedom," *Ensign*, November 1988, 8.

16. *True to the Faith*, 171.

17. See http://www.thefreedictionary.com/reincarnation.

CHAPTER 15: WHO WILL GO TO THE CELESTIAL KINGDOM?

1. Quentin L. Cook, "Our Father's Plan—Big Enough for All His Children," *Ensign*, May 2009, 37.

2. *Gospel Fundamentals* (Salt Lake City: The Church of Jesus Christ of Latter-day Saints, 1992), 220.

3. Joseph Fielding Smith, in Conference Report, April 1969, 122; emphasis added.

4. Russell M. Nelson, "Perfection Pending," *Ensign*, November 1995, 88.

5. Orson Pratt, in *Millennial Star* (November 17, 1866): 28:722.

6. Spencer W. Kimball, *The Teachings of Spencer W. Kimball*, ed. Edward L. Kimball (Salt Lake City: Bookcraft, 1982), 23.

7. Joseph Smith, *Teachings of the Prophet Joseph Smith*, comp. Joseph Fielding Smith (Salt Lake City: Deseret Book, 1976), 358.

8. Henry B. Eyring, "In the Strength of the Lord," *Ensign*, May 2004, 16.

CHAPTER 16: WHAT WILL WE BE LIKE WHEN WE'RE RESURRECTED?

1. *True to the Faith* (Salt Lake City: The Church of Jesus Christ of Latter-day Saints, 2004), 139.

2. *True to the Faith*, 115.

3. Joseph Fielding Smith, *Doctrines of Salvation: Sermons and Writings of Joseph Fielding Smith*, ed. Bruce R. McConkie, 3 vols. (Salt Lake City: Deseret Book, 1954–1956), 2:260; emphasis in original.

4. *"Preach My Gospel"* (Salt Lake City: The Church of Jesus Christ of Latter-day Saints, 2004), 59.

5. Smith, *Doctrines of Salvation*, 2:293.

6. James E. Talmage, in *Young Woman's Journal* 25 (October 1914): 603.

7. Spencer W. Kimball, *The Teachings of Spencer W. Kimball*, ed. Edward L. Kimball (Salt Lake City: Bookcraft, 1982), 36.

8. Joseph Smith, *The Words of Joseph Smith*, comp. and ed. Andrew F. Ehat and Lyndon W. Cook (Orem, Utah: Grandin Book Company, 1991), 370.

9. Joseph F. Smith, *Teachings of Presidents of the Church: Joseph F. Smith* (Salt Lake City: The Church of Jesus Christ of Latter-day Saints, 1998), 91.

10. Smith, *Doctrines of Salvation*, 2:286.

11. Smith, *Doctrines of Salvation*, 2:281; emphasis in original.

12. See http://10-most-common-phobias.com/common-phobias-home/10-most -common-phobias.

13. Smith, *Teachings of Presidents of the Church: Joseph F. Smith*, 89.

14. *True to the Faith*, 140.

Chapter 17: Our Final Judgment

1. See Robert L. Millet, Camille Fronk Olson, Andrew C. Skinner, and Brent L. Top, *LDS Beliefs: A Doctrinal Reference* (Deseret Book: Salt Lake City, 2011), 355.

2. Brad Wilcox, "His Grace Is Sufficient," BYU Devotional, July 12, 2011. http:// speeches.byu.edu/reader/reader.php?id=13436&x=59&y=9.

3. Dallin H. Oaks, "The Challenge to Become," *Ensign*, November 2000, 32.

4. *True to the Faith* (Salt Lake City: The Church of Jesus Christ of Latter-day Saints, 2004), 115.

5. J. Reuben Clark Jr., in Brigham Young University *Speeches of the Year*, May 3, 1955, 7.

6. David O. McKay, as quoted in Alexander B. Morrison, *Feed My Sheep: Leadership Ideas for Latter-day Shepherds* (Salt Lake City: Deseret Book, 1992), 156–57.

7. Dallin H. Oaks, "Preparation for the Second Coming," *Ensign*, May 2004, 9.

Conclusion: The Plan to Guide Our Everyday Lives

1. *For the Strength of Youth* (Salt Lake City: The Church of Jesus Christ of Latter-day Saints, 2011), 2.

2. Jeffrey R. Holland, "Personal Purity," *Ensign*, November 1998, 76.

3. "The Family: A Proclamation to the World," *Ensign*, November 1995, 102.

4. *Handbook 2: Administering the Church* (Salt Lake City: The Church of Jesus Christ of Latter-day Saints, 2010), 196.

5. *Handbook 2: Administering the Church*, 3.

6. Dallin H. Oaks, in "Same-Gender Attraction," http://newsroom.lds.org /official-statement/same-gender-attraction.

7. M. Russell Ballard, "Answers to Life's Questions," *Ensign*, May 1995, 24.

8. *True to the Faith* (Salt Lake City: The Church of Jesus Christ of Latter-day Saints, 2004), 115.

About the Authors

JOHN HILTON III is an assistant professor of ancient scripture at Brigham Young University. He has degrees from Brigham Young and Harvard Universities. John frequently speaks at Especially for Youth, Education Week, and Time Out for Women. He has published several titles with Deseret Book, including *The Little Book of Book of Mormon Evidences* and *Please Pass the Scriptures*. John and his wife, Lani, coauthored *What Guys Need to Know about Girls/What Girls Need to Know about Guys*. They are the parents of five children. For more information, please visit johnhiltoniii.com.

ANTHONY SWEAT is a full-time religious educator and received his PhD in education from Utah State University. He is a regular speaker at Especially for Youth, Education Week, Time Out for Women, and other LDS conferences. He is the author of several Deseret Book titles, including the best-selling *Mormons: An Open Book* and *I'm Not Perfect. Can I Still Go to Heaven?* He and his lovely wife, Cindy, are the parents of six children and reside in Utah. For more information, please visit anthonysweat.com.